Verse by Verse Commentary on the Letters of

JAMES
and
1-2 PETER

Enduring Word Commentary Series
By David Guzik

The grass withers, the flower fades,
but the word of our God stands forever.
Isaiah 40:8

Commentary on James and 1-2 Peter

Copyright ©2009 by David Guzik

Printed in the United States of America
or in the United Kingdom

ISBN 1-56599-028-5

Enduring Word Media

USA
5305 Woodbury
Ventura, CA 93003

Europe
Calvary Chapel Bibelschule
Eiserfelder Strasse 275
57080 Siegen
GERMANY
+49 (0)271 23 87 99 88

Electronic Mail: ewm@enduringword.com

Internet Home Page: www.enduringword.com

Scripture references, unless noted, are from the New King James Version of the Bible, copyright © 1979, 1980, 1982, Thomas Nelson, Inc., Publisher.

Table of Contents

Dedicated

to

Tony & Bobbye Moore

James 1 - A Living Faith in Trials and Temptations

A. Trials and wisdom.

1. (1) A Greeting from James.

James, a bondservant of God and of the Lord Jesus Christ,
To the twelve tribes which are scattered abroad: Greetings.

a. **James**: There are several men named **James** mentioned in the New Testament, but reliable tradition assigns this book to the one called *James the Just*, the half-brother of Jesus (Matthew 13:55) and the brother of Jude (Jude 1), who led the church in Jerusalem (Acts 15:13).

i. Other men mentioned in the Bible named **James** include:

- James, brother of John and son of Zebedee, the first apostle martyred and also known as *James the Less* (Matthew 10:2, Mark 15:40, Acts 12:2).

- James the son of Alphaeus, another of the twelve disciples (Matthew 10:3).

- James, the father of the "other" apostle Judas (Luke 6:16).

ii. Yet the writer of this letter is the same James who received a special resurrection appearance of Jesus (1 Corinthians 15:7). This was probably the cause of his conversion, because up to that time the brothers of Jesus seemed unsupportive of His message and mission (John 7:5).

iii. When he did follow Jesus, he followed with great devotion. An early history of the church says that James was such a man of prayer that his knees had large and thick calluses, making them look like the knees of a camel. It also says that James was martyred in Jerusalem by being pushed from a high point of the temple. Yet the fall did not kill him, and on the ground he was beaten to death, even as he prayed for his attackers.

b. **A bondservant of God and of the Lord Jesus Christ**: Knowing that this James was the half-brother of Jesus makes his self-introduction all the more significant. He did not proclaim himself "the brother of Jesus" but only **a bondservant of God and of the Lord Jesus Christ**. Jesus was more than James' brother; more importantly, Jesus was his **Lord**.

i. **Bondservant** is an important word. It translates the ancient Greek word *doulos*, and is probably better simply translated as *slave*. "A slave, a bondservant, one who is in a permanent relation of servitude to another . . . Among the Greeks, with their strong sense of personal freedom, the term carried a degrading connotation." (Hiebert)

ii. **Lord** is also an important word. It translates the ancient Greek word *kurios*. It simply meant the master of a *doulos*, and in the context it means that James considered Jesus *God*. "Hellenistic Jews used *Kurios* as a name for God; the non-use of the article gains in significance when it is remembered that *o Kurios*, 'Dominus,' was a title given to the early Roman Emperors in order to express their deity." (Oesterley in *Expositor's*)

c. **To the twelve tribes**: What James meant by this reference to **the twelve tribes** is difficult to understand. The question is whether James wrote a letter to only Christians from a Jewish background or to all Christians. Certainly this letter applies to all Christians; yet James probably wrote his letter before Gentiles were brought into the church, or at least before Gentile Christians appeared in any significant number.

i. **The twelve tribes** is a Jewish figure of speech that sometimes referred to the Jewish people as a whole (Matthew 19:28). Paul referred to *our twelve tribes* in his speech before King Agrippa (Acts 26:7). The concept of the "twelve tribes" among the Jewish people was still strong, even though they had not lived in their tribal allotments for centuries.

ii. In Galatians 2:8-9 Paul described some of the first-century apostles as *the apostleship to the circumcised*; that is to say they had their ministry mainly to the *lost sheep of Israel*, even as Jesus mentioned in Matthew 10:6 and 15:24. In the same context Paul mentioned this same **James**, so it is fair to also regard him as one having *the apostleship to the circumcised*.

iii. **Which are scattered abroad**: At this time, the Jewish people were scattered all over the world and there was a Christian presence among most Jewish communities throughout the world. Regarding the extent of the dispersion, Josephus wrote: "There is no city, no tribe, whether Greek or barbarian, in which Jewish law and Jewish customs have not taken root." (Cited in Barclay)

iv. Since this was written for the body of Christians as it existed at that time, this is also a letter for us today. Some think the book of James isn't important for Christians, and some quote Martin Luther's famous estimation of James as "a letter full of straw." But Luther's remark should be understood in its context. He was sometimes frustrated because those who wanted to promote salvation by works quoted certain verses from James against him. His intention was to observe that there was little or nothing in James that preached the gospel of justification by faith alone. In another place Luther wrote regarding James, "I think highly of the epistle of James, and regard it as valuable . . . It does not expound human doctrines, but lays much emphasis on God's law." (Cited in Barclay)

v. Martin Luther knew and taught exactly what the book of James teaches. The following is from his preface to Romans regarding saving faith: *O it is a living, busy active mighty thing, this faith. It is impossible for it not to be doing good things incessantly. It does not ask whether good works are to be done, but before the question is asked, it has already done this, and is constantly doing them. Whoever does not do such works, however, is an unbeliever. He gropes and looks around for faith and good works, but knows neither what faith is nor what good works are. Yet he talks and talks, with many words, about faith and good works.* (Cited in Moo)

vi. In many ways, we listen to the book of James because it echoes the teaching of Jesus. There are at least fifteen allusions to the Sermon on the Mount in James. A man who knew the teaching of Jesus and took it seriously wrote this letter.

d. **Greetings**: The salutation **Greetings** was the customary Greek way of opening a letter. Paul never used it; he preferred to salute his readers with the words *grace and peace*. Here James used this more customary salutation.

2. (2-4) Patient endurance in trials.

My brethren, count it all joy when you fall into various trials, knowing that the testing of your faith produces patience. But let patience have *its* perfect work, that you may be perfect and complete, lacking nothing.

a. **Count it all joy when you fall into various trials**: James regarded trials as inevitable. He said **when**, not *if* **you fall into various trials**. At the same time trials are occasions for **joy**, not discouraged resignation. We can **count it all joy** in the midst of trials because they are used to produce **patience**.

i. Moffatt translated James 1:2 as, *Greet it as pure joy*, pointing out a play on word between the *Greetings* at the end of James 1:1, and a similar word used to start James 1:2. It is "an attempt to bring out the play on words in the original, where the courteous *chairein* (greeting) is echoed by *charan* (joy)."

ii. The older King James Version says, *when ye fall into divers temptations*; but the rendering **trials** in the New King James Version is preferred. The word translated **trials** "signifies affliction, persecution, or *trial* of any kind; and in this sense it is used here, not intending diabolic suggestion, or what is generally understood by the word temptation." (Clarke)

iii. **When you fall into**: "Not go in step by step, but are precipitated, plunged. . . . When ye are so surrounded that there is no escaping them, being distressed, as David was, Psalm 116:3." (Trapp)

iv. **Patience** is the ancient Greek word *hupomone*. This word does not describe a passive waiting but an *active endurance*. It isn't so much the quality that helps you sit quietly in the doctor's waiting room, as it is the quality that helps you finish a marathon.

v. The ancient Greek word *hupomone* comes from *hupo* (under) and *meno* (to stay, abide, remain). At its root, it means *to remain under*. It has the picture of someone under a heavy load and choosing to stay there instead of trying to escape. The philosopher Philo called *hupomone* "the queen of virtues." (Cited in Hiebert) The Greek commentator Oesterley said this word **patience** described "the frame of mind which endures."

b. **Knowing that the testing of your faith produces patience**: Faith is *tested* through trials, not *produced* by trials. Trials reveal what faith we do have; not because God doesn't know how much faith we have, but so that our faith will be evident to ourselves and to those around us.

i. We notice that it is **faith** that is tested, and it shows that faith is important and precious – because only precious things are tested so thoroughly. "Faith is as vital to salvation as the heart is vital to the body: hence the javelins of the enemy are mainly aimed at this essential grace." (Spurgeon)

ii. If trials do not produce faith, what does? Romans 10:17 tells us: *So then faith comes by hearing, and hearing by the word of God.* Supernaturally, faith is built in us as we hear, understand, and trust in God's word.

iii. James did not want anyone to think that God sends trials to break down or destroy our faith; therefore, he will come back to this point in James 1:13-18.

c. **Produces patience**: Trials don't produce faith, but when trials are received with faith, it **produces patience**. Yet **patience** is not *inevitably* produced in times of trial. If difficulties are received in unbelief and grumbling, trials can produce bitterness and discouragement. This is why James exhorted us to **count it all joy**. Counting **it all joy** is faith's response to a time of trial.

> i. "It is occasionally asserted that James asks his readers to *enjoy* their trials . . . He did not say that they must *feel* it all joy, or that trials *are* all joy." (Hiebert)

d. **But let patience have its perfect work, that you may be perfect and complete, lacking nothing**: The work of patient endurance comes slowly and must be allowed to have full bloom. Patient endurance is a mark of the person who is **perfect and complete, lacking nothing**.

> i. "Patience must not be an inch shorter than the affliction. If the bridge reach but half-way over the brook, we shall have but ill-favoured passage. It is the devil's desire to set us on a hurry." (Trapp)

> ii. "These expressions in their present application are by some thought to be borrowed from the Grecian games: the man was *perfect*, who in any of the athletic exercises had got the victory; he was *entire*, having *everything complete*, who had the victory in the *pentathlon*, in each of the *five* exercises." (Clarke)

> iii. Others think that the terms come from the world of sacrifice, where only a potential sacrificial animal that was judged to be **perfect and complete, lacking nothing** was fit to offer God. It meant that the animal had been tested and approved.

> iv. "The natural tendency of trouble is not to sanctify, but to induce sin. A man is very apt to become unbelieving under affliction: that is a sin. He is apt to murmur against God under it: that is a sin. He is apt to put forth his hand to some ill way of escaping from his difficulty: and that would be sin. Hence we are taught to pray, 'Lead us not into temptation; because trial has in itself a measure of temptation'; and if it were not neutralized by abundant grace it would bear us towards sin." (Spurgeon)

> v. Yet, trials can prove a wonderful work of God in us. "I have looked back to times of trial with a kind of longing, not to have them return, but to feel the strength of God as I have felt it then, to feel the power of faith, as I have felt it then, to hang upon God's powerful arm as I hung upon it then, and to see God at work as I saw him then." (Spurgeon)

3. (5-8) How to receive the wisdom you need from God.

If any of you lacks wisdom, let him ask of God, who gives to all liberally and without reproach, and it will be given to him. But let him ask in faith, with no doubting, for he who doubts is like a wave of the sea driven and tossed by the wind. For let not that man suppose that he will

receive anything from the Lord; *he is* **a double-minded man, unstable in all his ways.**

a. **If any of you lacks wisdom**: Trials bring a necessary season to seek **wisdom** from God. We often don't know we need **wisdom** until our time of difficulty. Once in a time of trial, we need to know if a particular trial is something God wants us to eliminate by faith or persevere in by faith. This requires **wisdom**.

i. In trials, we need **wisdom** a lot more than we need *knowledge*. Knowledge is raw information but **wisdom** knows how to use it. Someone once said that knowledge is the ability to take things apart, but wisdom is the ability to put things together.

b. **Let him ask of God**: To receive wisdom, we simply **ask of God** - who gives wisdom generously (**liberally**), and without despising our request (**without reproach**).

i. "We are all so ready to go to books, to go to men, to go to ceremonies, to anything except to God. . . . Consequently, the text does not say, 'Let him ask books,' nor 'ask priests,' but, 'let him ask of God.'" (Spurgeon)

ii. God does indeed give **liberally**. "He gives according to his excellent greatness; as Alexander the Great gave a poor man a city; and when he modestly refused it as too great for him, Alexander answered, *Non quaero quid te accipere deceat, sed quid me dare*, The business is not what thou are fit to receive, but what it becometh me to give." (Trapp)

iii. **Without reproach**: "This is added, lest any one should fear to come too often to God . . . for he is ready ever to add new blessings to former ones, without any end or limitation." (Calvin) Knowing God's generosity – that He never despises or resents us for asking for wisdom – should encourage us to ask Him often. We understand that He is the God of the open hand, not the God of the clenched fist.

iv. When we want wisdom, the place to begin and end is the Bible. True wisdom will always be consistent with God's word.

v. The language here implies humility in coming to God. "It does not say, 'Let him buy of God, let him demand of God, let him earn from God.' Oh! No – 'let him ask of God.' It is the beggar's word. The beggar asks an alms. You are to ask as the beggar asks of you in the street, and God will give to you far more liberally than you give to the poor. You must confess that you have no merit of your own." (Spurgeon)

c. **But let him ask in faith**: Our request for wisdom must be made like any other request - **in faith**, without doubting God's ability or desire to give us His wisdom.

i. We notice that not only must one come in **faith**, but one must also **ask in faith**; and this is where the prayers of many people fail. "You know, dear friends, that there is a way of praying in which you ask for nothing, *and get it.*" (Spurgeon)

d. **With no doubting . . . let not that man suppose that he will receive anything from the Lord**: The one who doubts and lacks faith should not expect to receive **anything from the Lord**. This lack of faith and trust in God also shows that we have no foundation, being **unstable in all** our **ways**.

i. **Like a wave of the sea driven and tossed by the wind**: "The man who is not thoroughly persuaded that if he ask of God he shall receive, resembles a wave of the sea; he is in a state of continual agitation; driven by the wind, and tossed: now *rising* by *hope*, then *sinking* by *despair.*" (Clarke)

ii. **A wave of the sea** is a fitting description of one who is hindered by unbelief and unnecessary doubts.

- **A wave of the sea** is *without rest*, and so is the doubter
- **A wave of the sea** is *unstable*, and so is the doubter
- **A wave of the sea** is *driven by the winds*, and so is the doubter
- **A wave of the sea** is *capable of great destruction*, and so is the doubter

e. **A double-minded man, unstable in all his ways**: To ask God but to ask Him in a doubting way, shows that we are **double-minded**. If we had no faith, we would never ask at all. If we had no unbelief, we would have **no doubting**. To be in the middle ground between faith and unbelief is to be **double-minded**.

i. According to Hiebert, **double-minded** is literally *two-souled*. "The man of two souls, who has one for the earth, and another for heaven: who wishes to secure both worlds; he will not give up earth, and he is loath to let heaven go." (Clarke)

ii. The man who said to Jesus, "*Lord, I believe; help my unbelief!*" (Mark 9:24) was not **double-minded**. He wanted to believe, and declared his belief. His faith was weak, but it wasn't tinged with a **double-minded** doubt.

iii. "Do you believe that God can give you wisdom, and that he will do so if you ask him? Then, go at once to him, and say, 'Lord, this is what I need.' Specify your wants, state your exact condition, lay the whole case before God with as much orderliness as if you were telling your story to an intelligent friend who was willing to hear it, and prepared to help you; and then say, 'Lord, this is specifically what I think I want; and I ask this of thee believing that thou canst give it to me.'" (Spurgeon)

4. (9-11) Encouragement for those affected by trials.

Let the lowly brother glory in his exaltation, but the rich in his humiliation, because as a flower of the field he will pass away. For no sooner has the sun risen with a burning heat than it withers the grass; its flower falls, and its beautiful appearance perishes. So the rich man also will fade away in his pursuits.

a. **Let the lowly brother glory in his exaltation**: As much as it is appropriate for the **lowly** to rejoice when they are lifted up by God, so it is appropriate (but far more difficult) for the high (**the rich**) to rejoice when they are brought to **humiliation** by trials.

i. "As the poor brother forgets all his earthly poverty, so the rich brother forgets all his earthly riches. By faith in Christ the two are equals." (Hiebert, citing Lenski)

ii. Though we can understand the relative poverty and riches as trials or tests of a living faith that a Christian may deal with, it nonetheless seems that James has made a sudden shift in his subject, from trials and wisdom to riches and humility. In some ways, the Book of James is like the Book of Proverbs or other Old Testament wisdom literature, and it can jump from topic to topic and back again to a previous topic.

b. **Because as a flower of the field he will pass away**: Trials serve to remind the rich and the high that though they are comfortable in this life, it is still *only this life*, which fades as the grass grows brown and the flowers fade away.

i. In the land of Israel there are many kinds of beautiful flowers that spring to life when the rains come, but they last for only a short time before withering away. On the scale of eternity, this is how quickly **the rich man also will fade away in his pursuits**.

ii. The riches of this world will certainly **fade away** - but James says that the **rich man also will fade away**. If we put our life and our identity into things that **fade away**, we will **fade away** also. How much better to put our life and our identity into things that will never fade! If a man is only rich in this world, when he dies, he *leaves* his riches. But if a man is rich before God, when he dies, he *goes to* his riches.

B. Living for the Lord in times of temptation.

1. (12) A blessing for those who endure temptation.

Blessed *is* the man who endures temptation; for when he has been approved, he will receive the crown of life which the Lord has promised to those who love Him.

a. **Blessed is the man**: This sounds like one of Jesus' Beatitudes from the Sermon on the Mount (Matthew 5-7). In those great statements of blessing, Jesus did not tell us the *only* ways we can be **blessed**. Here we learn we can be **blessed** as we endure **temptation**.

    i. It does not say, "Blessed is the man who is never tempted." Nor does it say, "Blessed is the man who finds all temptation easy to conquer." Instead the promise of blessedness is given to the one who **endures temptation**. There is a special gift of blessedness from God to the one who can say "no" to temptation, thereby saying "yes" to God.

b. **For when he has been approved**: Here James states the purpose of God in allowing temptation. The purpose is to *approve* us; that through the testing we would be revealed as genuine and strong in our faith.

c. **Who endures temptation**: **Temptation** is one of the *various trials* (James 1:2) we face. As we persevere through temptation, we are **approved**, and will be rewarded as the work of God in us is evident through our resistance of temptation.

d. **The crown of life which the Lord has promised**: James reminds us that it really is *worth it* to endure under the temptations we face. Our steadfastness will be rewarded as we demonstrate our **love** for Jesus (**to those who love Him**) by resisting temptation.

    i. "There is a crown for me. . . . Then will I gird up my loins and quicken my pace, since the crown is so sure to those who run with patience." (Spurgeon)

e. **To those who love Him**: This describes the *motive* for resisting temptation, because of our love for God. The passions of sinful temptation can only really be overcome by a greater passion, and that is a passion for the honor and glory and relationship with God.

    i. Some resist temptation because of the fear of man. The thief suddenly becomes honest when he sees a policeman. The man or woman controls their lusts because they couldn't bear to be found out and thus embarrassed. Others resist the temptation to one sin because of the power of another sin. The greedy miser gives up partying because he doesn't want to spend the money. But the best motive for resisting temptation is to **love Him**; to **love Him** with greater power and greater passion than your love for the sin.

    ii. "So that those who endure temptation rightly, endure it because they love God. They say to themselves, 'How can I do this great wickedness, and sin against God?' They cannot fall into sin because it would grieve him who loves them so well, and whom they love with all their hearts." (Spurgeon)

2. (13-16) How temptation comes and works.

Let no one say when he is tempted, "I am tempted by God"; for God cannot be tempted by evil, nor does He Himself tempt anyone. But each one is tempted when he is drawn away by his own desires and enticed. Then, when desire has conceived, it gives birth to sin; and sin, when it is full-grown, brings forth death. Do not be deceived, my beloved brethren.

a. **Let no one say when he is tempted, "I am tempted by God"**: Temptation does not come from God. Though He allows it, He Himself does not entice us to evil, though God may test our faith *without* a solicitation to evil (**nor does He Himself tempt anyone**).

    i. James knew that most people have an evil tendency to blame God when they find themselves in trials. Yet by His very nature, God is *unable* to either be tempted (in the sense we are tempted, as James will explain), **nor does He Himself tempt anyone.**

    ii. "He shows the great cause of sin; that lust hath a greater hand in it than either the devil or his instruments, who cannot make us sin without ourselves: they sometimes tempt, and do not prevail." (Poole)

    iii. God sometimes allows great tests to come to His people, even some who might be thought of as His favorites. We think of the hard command He gave to Abraham (Genesis 22:1), and the affliction He allowed to come to Job (Job 1-2). Other times He may send tests as a form of judgment upon those who have rejected Him, such as sending a spirit to bring deception (1 Kings 22:19-23) or departing from a man and refusing to answer him (1 Samuel 28:15-16). Yet in no case does God entice a person to evil.

    iv. "Satan tempts: God tries. But the same trial may be both a temptation and a trial; and it may be a trial from God's side, and a temptation from Satan's side, just as Job suffered from Satan, and it was a temptation; but he also suffered from God through Satan, and so it was a trial to him." (Spurgeon)

b. **Each one is tempted when he is drawn away by his own desires and enticed**: God doesn't tempt us. Instead, temptation comes when we are **drawn away** by our own fleshly **desires** and **enticed** - with the world and the devil providing the enticement.

    i. **Drawn away**: "It is either a metaphor taken from a fish enticed by a bait, and drawn after it, or rather from a harlot drawing a young man out of the right way, and alluring him with the bait of pleasure to commit folly with her." (Poole)

ii. Satan certainly tempts us, but the only reason temptation has a hook in us is because of our own fallen nature, which corrupts our God-given **desires**. We often give Satan too much credit for his tempting powers and fail to recognize that we are **drawn away by** our **own desires**. Some people practically beg Satan to tempt them.

iii. Some who like to emphasize the sovereignty of God say that God is responsible for all things. Yet God is never responsible for man's sin. In his commentary on this text, John Calvin himself wrote, "When Scripture ascribes blindness or hardness of heart to God, it does not assign to him the beginning of the blindness, nor does it make him the author of sin, so as to ascribe to him the blame." Calvin also wrote, "Scripture asserts that the reprobate are delivered up to depraved lusts; but is it because the Lord depraves or corrupts their hearts? By no means; for their hearts are subjected to depraved lusts, because they are already corrupt and vicious."

c. **When desire has conceived, it gives birth to sin**: Springing forth from corrupt **desire** is **sin**. Springing forth from **sin** is **death**. This progression to death is an inevitable result that Satan always tries to hide from us, but we should never be deceived about.

i. "James represents men's *lust* as a *harlot*, which entices their understanding and will into its impure embraces, and from that conjunction *conceives* sin. Sin, being *brought forth*, immediately acts, and is nourished by frequent repetition, until at length it gains such strength that in its turn it *begets* death. This is the true *genealogy* of sin and death." (Clarke)

d. **Do not be deceived, my beloved brethren**: Satan's great strategy in temptation is to convince us that the pursuit of our corrupt desires will somehow produce life and goodness for us. If we remember that Satan only comes *to steal, and to kill, and to destroy* (John 10:10), then we can more effectively resist the deceptions of temptation.

3. (17-18) God's goodness stands in contrast to the temptations we face.

Every good gift and every perfect gift is from above, and comes down from the Father of lights, with whom there is no variation or shadow of turning. Of His own will He brought us forth by the word of truth, that we might be a kind of firstfruits of His creatures.

a. **Every good gift and every perfect gift is from above**: We expect no true goodness from our own fallen natures and from those who would entice us. But **every good and every perfect gift** comes from God the Father in heaven.

i. Of course, the ultimate goodness of any gift must be measured on an eternal scale. Something that may seem to be only good (such as winning money in a lottery) may in fact be turned to our destruction.

b. **With whom there is no variation or shadow of turning**: God's goodness is constant. There is **no variation** with Him. Instead of shadows, God is **the Father of lights**.

i. According to Hiebert, the ancient Greek is actually "the Father of *the* lights." The specific **lights** are the celestial bodies that light up the sky, both day and night. The sun and stars never stop giving light, even when we can't see them. Even so, there is never a **shadow** with God. When night comes, the darkness isn't the fault of the sun; it shines as brightly as before. Instead, the earth has turned from the sun and darkness comes.

ii. This means that God never changes. Among modern theologians, there are some that are taken with something called *process theology*, which says that God is "maturing" and "growing" and "in process" Himself. Yet the Bible says that **there is no variation or shadow of turning** with God.

c. **Of His own will He brought us forth by the word of truth**: James understood that the gift of salvation was given by God, and not earned by the work or obedience of man. It is **of His own will** that **He brought us forth** for salvation.

i. **He brought us forth**: "The word properly signifies, He did the office of a mother to us, the bringing us into the light of life." (Trapp)

ii. "Now mostly, men who are generous need to have their generosity excited. They will need to be waited upon; appeals must be laid before them; they must sometimes be pressed; an example must lead them on. But 'of his own will' God did to us all that has been done, without any incentive or prompting, moved only by himself, because he delighteth in mercy; because his name and his nature are love because evermore, like the sun, it is natural to him to distribute the beams of his eternal grace." (Spurgeon)

d. **That we might be a kind of firstfruits of His creatures**: We can see God's goodness in our salvation, as He initiated our salvation **of His own will** and **brought us forth** to spiritual life by His **word of truth**, that we might be to His glory as **firstfruits** of His harvest.

i. In the previous verses James told us what the lust of man brings forth: sin and death. Here he tells us what the **will** of the good God brings: salvation to us, as **a kind of firstfruits of His creatures**.

ii. James may refer to his own generation of believers when he calls them **firstfruits**, especially as being mainly written to Christians from a Jewish background. The fact that these Christians from a Jewish background are **firstfruits** (Deuteronomy 26:1-4) shows that James expected a subsequent and greater harvest of Christians from a Gentile background.

iii. Some have speculated on the idea of **firstfruits of His creatures** even more (perhaps too far), saying that James had in mind a wider redemption among unknown creatures of God, of which we are the **firstfruits** of that wider redemption.

4. (19-20) Standing firm against unrighteous anger.

So then, my beloved brethren, let every man be swift to hear, slow to speak, slow to wrath; for the wrath of man does not produce the righteousness of God.

a. **Let every man be swift to hear, slow to speak, slow to wrath**: We can learn to be **slow to wrath** by first learning to be **swift to hear** and **slow to speak**. Much of our anger and wrath comes from being *self-centered* and not *others-centered*. **Swift to hear** is a way to be *others-centered*. **Slow to speak** is a way to be *others-centered*.

i. "But hath not Nature taught us the same that the apostle here doth, by giving us two ears, and those open; and but one tongue, and that hedged in with teeth and lips?" (Trapp)

b. **Slow to wrath; for the wrath of man does not produce the righteousness of God**: In light of the nature of temptation and the goodness of God, we must take special care to be **slow to wrath**, because our wrath does not accomplish the **righteousness of God**. Our **wrath** almost always simply defends or promotes our own agenda.

5. (21) Standing firm against the lusts of the flesh.

Therefore lay aside all filthiness and overflow of wickedness, and receive with meekness the implanted word, which is able to save your souls.

a. **All filthiness and overflow of wickedness**: This has in mind an impure manner of living. In light of the nature of temptation and the goodness of God, we are to **lay aside all** impurity, putting them far from us.

i. **All filthiness**: "The stinking filth of a pestilent ulcer. Sin is the devil's vomit, the soul's excrement, the superfluity or garbage of naughtiness [**wickedness**] . . . as it is here called by an allusion to the garbage of the sacrifices cast into the brook Kedron, that is, the town-ditch." (Trapp)

ii. The older King James Version translates the phrase **overflow of wickedness** as *superfluity of naughtiness*.

b. **Receive with meekness the implanted word**: In contrast to an impure manner of living, we should **receive the implanted word** of God (doing it **with meekness**, a teachable heart). This word is **able to save** us, both in our current situation and eternally. The purity of God's word can preserve us even in an impure age.

   i. "The first thing, then, is *receive*. That word 'receive' is a very instructive gospel word; it is the door through which God's grace enters to us. We are not saved by working, but by receiving; not by what we give to God, but by what God gives to us, and we receive from him." (Spurgeon)

   ii. Here James alluded to the spiritual power of the word of God. When it is **implanted** in the human heart, it is **able to save your souls**. The word of God carries the power of God.

6. (22-25) How to receive the word of God.

But be doers of the word, and not hearers only, deceiving yourselves. For if anyone is a hearer of the word and not a doer, he is like a man observing his natural face in a mirror; for he observes himself, goes away, and immediately forgets what kind of man he was. But he who looks into the perfect law of liberty and continues *in it*, and is not a forgetful hearer but a doer of the work, this one will be blessed in what he does.

a. **But be doers of the word, and not hearers only**: We must receive God's word as **doers**, not merely **hearers**. To take comfort in the fact you have heard God's word when you haven't *done* it is to deceive yourself.

   i. It was common in the ancient world for people to hear a teacher. If you followed the teacher and tried to *live* what he said, you were called a *disciple* of that teacher. We may say that Jesus is looking for disciples: doers, not mere hearers.

   ii. Jesus used this same point to conclude His great Sermon on the Mount. He said that the one who heard the word without doing it was like a man who built his house on the sand, but the one who heard God's word and did it was like a man whose house was built on a rock. The one who both heard and did God's word could withstand the inevitable storms of life and the judgment of eternity (Matthew 7:24-27).

   iii. "A teacher or preacher may give an eloquent address on the gospel, or explain ably some O.T. prophecy about Christ, but when the sermon is done, it is not done; something remains to be done by the hearers in life, and if they content themselves with sentimental admiration or with enjoying the emotional or mental treat, they need not imagine that this is religion." (Moffatt)

iv. "I fear we have many such in all congregations; admiring hearers, affectionate hearers, attached hearers, but all the while unblest hearers, because they are not doers of the word." (Spurgeon)

v. "You know the old story; I am half ashamed to repeat it again, but it is so pat to the point. When Donald came out of kirk sooner than usual, Sandy said to him, 'What, Donald, is the sermon all done?' 'No,' said Donald, 'it is all said, but it is not begun to be done yet.'" (Spurgeon)

b. **He is like a man observing his natural face in a mirror; for he observes himself, goes away, and immediately forgets what kind of man he was**: The person who only hears God's word without doing it has the same sense and stability as a man who looks into a mirror and immediately forgets what he saw. The information he received did not do any good in his life.

i. **Observing his natural face**: The ancient Greek word translated **observing** has the idea of *a careful scrutiny*. By application, James had in mind people who give *a careful scrutiny* of God's word; they may be regarded as Bible experts but it still doesn't result in *doing*.

ii. "The glass of the Word is not like our ordinary looking-glass, which merely shows us our external features; but, according to the Greek of our text, the man sees in it 'the face of his birth'; that is, the face of his nature. He that reads and hears the Word may see not only his actions there, but his motives, his desires, his inward condition." (Spurgeon)

iii. Understanding this power of the Word of God, the preacher is responsible for working hard to not hinder this power. "Certain preachers dream that it is their business to paint pretty pictures: but it is not so. We are not to design and sketch, but simply to give the reflection of truth. We are to hold up the mirror to nature in a moral and spiritual sense, and let men see themselves therein. We have not even to make the mirror, but only to hold it up. The thoughts of God, and not our own thoughts, are to be set before our hearers' minds; and these discover a man to himself. The Word of the Lord is a revealer of secrets: it shows a man his life, his thoughts, his heart, his inmost self." (Spurgeon)

iv. A healthy person looks in the mirror to *do* something, not just to admire the image. Even so, a healthy Christian looks into God's Word to *do* something about it, not just to store up facts that he will not put to use by being a **doer** of the word.

v. "The *doctrines of God*, faithfully preached, are such a *mirror*; he who hears cannot help discovering his own character, and being affected with his own deformity; he sorrows, and purposes amendment; but when the preaching is over, the mirror is removed . . . he soon forgets what manner of man he was . . . he reasons himself out of the necessity of repentance and amendment of life, and thus deceives his soul." (Clarke)

vi. "Get thee God's law as a glass to toot [to study carefully] in, saith Mr. Bradford; so shalt thou see thy face foul arrayed, and so shamefully saucy, mangy, pocky, and scabbed, that thou canst not but be sorry at the contemplation thereof." (Trapp)

c. **But he who looks into the perfect law of liberty and continues in it . . . this one will be blessed in what he does**: If we study the Word of God intently, and do it (**continue in it**), then we will be **blessed**.

i. **He who looks into the perfect law of liberty**: In the ancient Greek language, the word for **looks into** spoke of a penetrating examination, so that a person would even bend over to get a better look. Though James stressed *doing*, he did not neglect *studying* God's Word either. We should *look into* God's Word.

ii. Adam Clarke points out that the ancient Greek word translated **continues** is *parameinas* and has this sense: "Takes time to see and examine the state of his soul, the grace of his God, the extent of his duty, and the height of the promised glory. The metaphor here is taken from those females who spend much time at their glass, in order that they may decorate themselves to the greatest advantage, and not leave one hair, or the smallest ornament, out of its place."

iii. **The perfect law of liberty**: This is a wonderful way to describe the Word of God. In the New Covenant, God reveals to us a **law**, but it is a **law of liberty**, written on our transformed hearts by the Spirit of God.

iv. "The whole doctrine of Scripture, or especially the gospel, called a *law*, Romans 3:27, both as it is a rule, and by reason of the power it hath over the heart; and a *law of liberty*, because it shows the way to the best liberty, freedom from sin, the bondage of the ceremonial law, the rigour of the moral, and from the wrath of God." (Poole)

7. (26-27) Examples of what it means to be a doer of the Word of God.

If anyone among you thinks he is religious, and does not bridle his tongue but deceives his own heart, this one's religion *is* useless. Pure and undefiled religion before God and the Father is this: to visit orphans and widows in their trouble, *and* to keep oneself unspotted from the world.

a. **If anyone among you thinks he is religious**: James just explained that real religion is not shown by hearing the word, but by doing it. One way to do God's word is to **bridle** the **tongue**.

i. **Thinks he is religious**: The New Testament never uses this ancient Greek word for "**religious**" in a positive sense (Acts 17:22, 25:19, 26:5; Colossians 2:23). James used it here of someone who is **religious**, but is not really right with God, and this is evident because he **does not bridle his tongue**.

b. **This one's religion is useless**: Your walk with God **is useless** if it does not translate into the way you live and the way you treat others. Many are deceived in their own heart regarding the reality of their walk with God.

i. "This seems to reflect upon the hypocritical Jews, whose religion consisted so much in external observances, and keeping themselves from ceremonial defilements, when yet they were sullied with so many moral ones, James 1:14; Matthew 23:23; John 18:28; devoured widows' houses." (Poole)

ii. "He does not deny the place of public worship (see James 2:2, 5:14) or of religious observances, but he explains that in God's sight a **pure, unsoiled religion** expresses itself in acts of charity and in chastity – the two features of early Christian ethics which impressed the contemporary world." (Moffatt)

c. **Pure and undefiled religion before God**: There is a great deal of pure and undefiled religion *in the sight of man* that is not **pure and undefiled religion before God**.

d. **To visit orphans and widows in their trouble, and to keep oneself unspotted from the world**: A real walk with God shows itself in simple, practical ways. It helps the needy and keeps itself unstained by the world's corruption.

i. "The Biblical Ritualism, the pure external worship, the true embodiment of the inward principles of religion is to visit the fatherless and widows in their affliction, and to keep ourselves unspotted from the world. Charity and purity are the two great garments of Christianity." (Spurgeon)

ii. "True religion does not merely *give* something for the *relief* of the distressed, but it *visits them*, it takes the *oversight of them*, it takes them under its care; so *episkeptesthai* means. It goes to their houses, and speaks to their hearts; it relieves their wants, sympathizes with them in their distresses, instructs them in divine things, and recommends them to God. And all this it does for the Lord's sake. This is the religion of Christ." (Clarke)

e. **Unspotted from the world**: The idea is not that a Christian retreats away from the world; instead they interact with **orphans and widows in their trouble** and others such in their need. The Christian ideal is not to retreat from the world; they are in the world, they are not *of* it; and remain **unspotted from the world**.

i. "I would like to see a Christian, not kept in a glass case away from trial and temptation, but yet covered with an invisible shield, so that, wherever he went, he would be guarded and protected from the evil influences that are in the world in almost every place." (Spurgeon)

ii. From the book of Genesis, Lot is an example of a man who *was* spotted by the world. He started living *towards* Sodom, disregarding the spiritual climate of the area because of the prosperity of the area. Eventually he moved to the wicked city and became a part of the city's leadership. The end result was that Lot lost *everything* - and was saved as only by the skin of his teeth.

iii. "There is no book with so lofty an ideal of what life may become when it is yielded to the grace of Christ. A cleansed heart, and an unspotted robe; no sin allowed and permitted in the soul, and no evil habit allowed to dominate and enthrall the life." (Meyer)

James 2 - A Living Faith in the Life of the Church

A. Partiality and discrimination in the family of God.

1. (1) The principle established.

My brethren, do not hold the faith of our Lord Jesus Christ, *the Lord of glory,* **with partiality.**

a. **Do not hold the faith**: The glorious **faith** we have, the **faith of our Lord Jesus Christ**, should never be associated **with partiality** (discrimination). The **Lord of glory** Himself shows no partiality (Deuteronomy 10:17 and Acts 10:34) so neither should those who put their trust in Him.

i. James used strong words to refer to Jesus Christ: **The Lord of glory**. Moffatt comments: "The Christian religion [is here called] more explicitly **belief in the Lord Jesus Christ, who is the divine Glory** – a striking term for Christ as the full manifestation of the divine presence and majesty. The Jews called this the *shekinah*."

ii. This is especially significant because James is widely (and properly) regarded as one of the first letters of the New Testament written (perhaps somewhere between AD 44 and 48). This means that the *earliest* Christians considered Jesus to be God, and said so in strong, unmistakable words.

b. **With partiality**: We do well to remember that James wrote to a very partial age, filled with prejudice and hatred based on class, ethnicity, nationality, and religious background. In the ancient world people were routinely and permanently categorized because they were Jew or Gentile, slave or free, rich or poor, Greek or barbarian, or whatever.

i. A significant aspect of the work of Jesus was to break down these walls that divided humanity, and to bring forth one new race of mankind in Him (Ephesians 2:14-15).

ii. The unity and openness of the early church was shocking to the ancient world. But this unity didn't come automatically. As this command from James shows, the apostles had to teach the early church to never **hold the faith of our Lord Jesus Christ . . . with partiality**.

2. (2-4) An example of the kind of partiality that has no place among Christians.

For if there should come into your assembly a man with gold rings, in fine apparel, and there should also come in a poor man in filthy clothes, and you pay attention to the one wearing the fine clothes and say to him, "You sit here in a good place," and say to the poor man, "You stand there," or, "Sit here at my footstool," have you not shown partiality among yourselves, and become judges with evil thoughts?

a. **If there should come into your assembly**: In the ancient Greek, the word **assembly** is literally *synagogue*, the name of the meeting place for Jews. The fact that James calls a *Christian* meeting place a *synagogue* shows that he wrote before Gentiles were widely received into the church. At the time James wrote, most all Christians came from a Jewish heritage. This is the only place in the New Testament where an **assembly** of Christians is clearly called a *synagogue*.

i. "Till the final rift between Judaism and Christianity both Christian and non-Christian Jews used, at least often, the same word for their sacred meeting-place." (Adamson)

ii. "As Christians have no church-buildings at this period, their place of **meeting** was usually some large room in the house of a wealthy member or a hall hired for the purpose (Acts 19:9), where outsiders were free to attend the ordinary services . . . They were to be welcomed, but welcomed without any servility or snobbery." (Moffatt)

b. **A man with gold rings**: This showed the man was rich. "In Roman society the wealthy wore rings on their left hand in great profusion. A sign of wealth, rings were worn with great ostentation. There were even shops in Rome where rings could be rented for special occasions." (Hiebert)

i. **There should also come in a poor man**: "The word signifies one very poor, even to beggarliness." (Poole)

c. **Have you not shown partiality among yourselves, and become judges with evil thoughts?** To favor the **rich man** over the **poor man** in the way James described shows a deep carnality among Christians. Their **evil thoughts** are evident by their partial actions.

i. To show **partiality** shows that we care more for the outward appearance than we do upon the heart. *For the Lord does not see as man sees; for man looks at the outward appearance, but the* LORD *looks at the heart* (1 Samuel 16:7). God looks at the heart, and so should we.

ii. To show **partiality** shows that we misunderstand who is important and blessed in the sight of God. When we assume that the rich man is more important to God or more blessed by God, we put too much value in material riches.

iii. To show **partiality** shows a selfish streak in us. Usually we favor the **rich man** over the **poor man** because we believe we can get more from the **rich man**. He can do favors for us that the **poor man** can't.

3. (5-7) Man's partiality rarely agrees with God's heart.

Listen, my beloved brethren: Has God not chosen the poor of this world
***to be* rich in faith and heirs of the kingdom which He promised to those who love Him? But you have dishonored the poor man. Do not the rich oppress you and drag you into the courts? Do they not blaspheme that noble name by which you are called?**

a. **Has God not chosen the poor of this world to be rich in faith and heirs of the kingdom**: Though it is easy for man to be partial to the rich, God isn't partial to them. In fact, since riches are an obstacle to the kingdom of God (Matthew 19:24), there is a sense in which God specially blesses the poor of this world.

i. They are **chosen . . . to be rich in faith** because the **poor of this world** simply have more opportunities to trust God. Therefore they may be far more **rich in faith** than the rich man. "The rich man may trust Him; but the poor man must. . . . the poor man has no fortress in which to hide, except the two strong arms of God." (Meyer)

ii. "This seems to refer to Matthew 11:5: *And the poor have the Gospel preached to them.* These believed on the Lord Jesus, and found his salvation; while the *rich* despised, neglected, and persecuted him." (Clarke)

b. **Has not God chosen**: The poor are **chosen** in the sense that the poor more readily respond to God in faith, having fewer obstacles to the kingdom.

i. "Church history demonstrates that comparatively more poor people than rich have responded to the gospel." (Hiebert)

ii. When we choose people by what we can see on the surface, we miss the mind of God. Remember that Judas *appeared* to be much better leadership material than Peter.

iii. What is more, we can say that God has **chosen the poor** in the sense that when He added humanity to His deity and came to earth, He came into poverty. "There is nothing that men dread more than poverty. They will break every commandment in the Decalogue rather than be poor. But it is God's chosen lot. He had one opportunity only of living our life, and He chose to be born of parents too poor to present more than two doves at his presentation in the temple." (Meyer)

iv. Of course, God has not *only* **chosen the poor**. Yet we may say that He has **chosen the poor** first, in the sense Paul spoke of in 1 Corinthians 1:26: *For you see your calling, brethren, that not many wise according to the flesh, not many mighty, not many noble, are called.* "Not that God hath chosen all the poor in the world, but his choice is chiefly of them." (Poole)

v. Calvin wrote regarding God's choice of the poor: "Not indeed alone, but he wished to begin with them, that he might beat down the pride of the rich."

vi. We should remind ourselves that God also never calls for partiality *against* the rich. If one must judge in a dispute between a rich man and a poor man, they should let the law and the facts of the case decide the judgment instead of the economic class of those in the dispute.

c. **Do not the rich oppress you and drag you into the courts?** James reminded his readers that the rich often sin against them (**oppress you . . . drag you**). This is often because the love of money is the root of every kind of evil (1 Timothy 6:10). For this reason alone, the rich are not worthy of the partiality often shown to them.

i. History shows that the rich can indeed oppress the poor. "Trample upon you with the feet of pride and cruelty; yea, devour you, as the greater fish do the lesser. . . . This is a sin against race, grace, and place." (Trapp)

ii. **Do they not blaspheme**: "If the rich here spoken of were Christians, then they may be said to blaspheme Christ's name, when by their wicked carriage they caused it to be blasphemed by others . . . but if rich unbelievers be here meant, the rich men of those times being generally great enemies to Christianity." (Poole)

4. (8-9) Partiality is condemned by the Scriptures.

If you really fulfill *the* royal law according to the Scripture, "You shall love your neighbor as yourself," you do well; but if you show partiality, you commit sin, and are convicted by the law as transgressors.

a. **If you really fulfill the royal law according to the Scripture**: James anticipated that some of his readers might defend their partiality to the rich as simply loving the rich man as their neighbor in obedience to the law.

b. **If you show partiality, you commit sin**: The problem isn't that one is nice to the rich. The problem is that one does **show partiality** to the rich, and is not nice to the poor man! So you can't excuse your **partiality** by saying, "I'm just fulfilling the command to love my neighbor as myself."

c. **The royal law**: Our God is a great King, and His law is a **royal law**. Our King Jesus put special emphasis on this command (Matthew 22:36-40) from the Old Testament (Leviticus 19:18). James is reminding us that the poor man is just as much our **neighbor** as the rich man is.

> i. "This commandment, *Thou shalt love thy neighbour as thyself*, is a *royal law*, not only because it is ordained of God, and proceeds from his *kingly* authority over men, but because it is so *useful, suitable,* and *necessary* to the present state of man . . . we give the epithet *royal* to whatever is excellent, noble, grand, or useful." (Clarke)

5. (10-13) The serious matter of obeying all of God's commands.

For whoever shall keep the whole law, and yet stumble in one *point*, he is guilty of all. For He who said, "Do not commit adultery," also said, "Do not murder." Now if you do not commit adultery, but you do murder, you have become a transgressor of the law. So speak and so do as those who will be judged by the law of liberty. For judgment is without mercy to the one who has shown no mercy. Mercy triumphs over judgment.

a. **Whoever shall keep the whole law, and yet stumble in one point, he is guilty of all**: James here guards us against a selective obedience, the sort that will pick and choose which commands of God should be obeyed and which can be safely disregarded.

> i. We can't say, "I like God's command against murder, so I'll keep that one. But I don't like His command against adultery, so I will disregard it." God cares about the **whole law**.

> ii. The **whole law** must be kept if one will be justified by the law. "In the tract *Shabbath*, fol. 70, where they dispute concerning the thirty-nine works commanded by Moses, Rabbi Yochanan says: *But if a man do the whole, with the omission of one, he is guilty of the whole, with the one.*" (Clarke) Adamson quotes one ancient Rabbi who taught: "If a man perform all the commandments, save one, he is guilty of all and each; to break one precept is to defy God who commanded the whole."

> iii. "He breaks the whole law, though not the whole of the law: as he that wounds a man's arm wounds the whole man, though not the whole of the man." (Poole)

b. **So speak and so do as those who will be judged by the law of liberty**: We are under the **law of liberty**. It has **liberty**, yet it is still a **law** that must be obeyed and that we will be judged by at the judgment seat of Christ (2 Corinthians 5:10).

> i. "It is also called a law of liberty, because it is freely and willingly kept of the regenerate, to whom it is no burden or bondage." (Trapp)

c. **For judgment is without mercy to the one who has shown no mercy**: As those who **will be judged by the law of liberty**, we should always show **mercy** to others by refraining from partiality. The mercy we show will be extended to us again on the day of judgment, and that **mercy triumphs over judgment**.

i. James is relating another principle of Jesus from the Sermon on the Mount: *For with what judgment you judge, you will be judged; and with the measure you use, it will be measured back to you* (Matthew 7:2).

ii. "The law of liberty is the law which defines our relationship to God and man as love-mastered. To speak and do under that impulse, is to be free indeed. If that law be disobeyed, if no mercy be shown, then judgment based upon that law will show no mercy." (Morgan)

iii. "The **law of freedom** is not laxity but a strict ethical rule of God, and we shall be **judged** by our adherence to its supreme principle of brotherly love or **mercy**, i.e. compassion for the sins and sufferings of our fellows." (Moffatt)

iv. **Mercy triumphs over judgment**: Moffatt translates this, "The merciful life will triumph in the face of judgment." "That is, the merciful man glorieth, as one that hath received mercy, and shall not come into condemnation; for God's mercy rejoiceth against such a man's sins, as against an adversary which he hath subdued and trampled on." (Trapp)

B. The demonstration of a living faith in loving action.

1. (14) The principle established: true faith will be accompanied by action.

What *does it* profit, my brethren, if someone says he has faith but does not have works? Can faith save him?

a. **What does it profit, my brethren**: James thought it impossible that someone could genuinely have saving faith with no works. But someone could *say* **he has faith**, but fail to show good works. So, the question is valid: **Can** *that kind* of **faith save him**?

i. "The apostle had just before declared, that they who are unmerciful to men shall find God severe to themselves, and have judgment without mercy: but hypocritical professors boasted of their faith as sufficient to secure them against that judgment, though they neglected the practice of holiness and righteousness." (Poole)

b. **Someone says he has faith but does not have works**: James wrote to Christians from a Jewish background that discovered the glory of salvation by faith. They knew the exhilaration of freedom from works-righteousness. But they then went to the other extreme of thinking that **works** didn't matter at all.

c. **Can faith save him?** James did not contradict the Apostle Paul, who insisted that we are saved *not of works* (Ephesians 2:9). James merely clarifies for us the *kind of faith that saves*. We are saved by grace through faith, not by works; but saving faith will have works that accompany it. As a saying goes: *faith alone saves, but the faith that saves is not alone*; it has good works with it.

i. Paul also understood the necessity of works in proving the character of our faith. He wrote: *For we are His workmanship, created in Christ Jesus for good works, which God prepared beforehand that we should walk in them* (Ephesians 2:10). He also wrote: *This is a faithful saying, and these things I want you to affirm constantly, that those who have believed in God should be careful to maintain good works.* (Titus 3:8)

ii. **Can faith save him?** "That is, his profession of faith; for it is not said that he *has faith*, but that *he says*, I have faith." (Clarke)

2. (15-17) An example of dead faith.

If a brother or sister is naked and destitute of daily food, and one of you says to them, "Depart in peace, be warmed and filled," but you do not give them the things which are needed for the body, what *does it* profit? Thus also faith by itself, if it does not have works, is dead.

a. **If a brother or sister is naked and destitute of daily food**: To fail in the most simple good work towards a brother or sister in need demonstrates that one does not have a living faith, and we can only be saved by a living faith in Jesus.

i. "Under these two of nakedness and hunger, he comprehends all the calamities of human life, which may be relieved by the help of others; as food and raiment contain all the ordinary supports and comforts of life, Genesis 28:20; Matthew 6:25; 1 Timothy 6:8." (Poole)

b. **Be warmed and filled**: To say this means you know that the person in front of you *needs* clothing and food. You know their need well, but offer nothing to help them except a few religious words.

i. "How many have we now-a-days that will be but as friends at a sneeze! The most you can get out of these benefactors is, 'God bless you, Christ help you.'" (Trapp)

c. **What does it profit?** Real faith, and the works that accompany it, are not made up of only spiritual things, but also of a concern for the most basic needs - such as the need for comfort, covering, and food. When needs arise, we should sometimes *pray* less, and simply *do more* to help the person in need. We can sometimes *pray* as a substitute for *action*.

i. "Your pretending to have faith, while you have no works of charity or mercy, is utterly vain: for as *faith*, which is a principle in the mind, cannot be discerned but by the *effects*, that is, *good works*; he who has no good works has, presumptively, no faith." (Clarke)

d. **Thus also faith by itself, if it does not have works, is dead**: This is the first time James speaks of a **dead** faith. Faith alone saves us, but it must be a *living faith*. We can tell if faith is *alive* by seeing if it is accompanied by **works**, and **if it does not have works**, **it is dead**.

i. A *living faith* is simply *real faith*. If we really believe something we will follow through and act upon it. If we really put our trust and faith on Jesus, we will care for the **naked and destitute** as He told us to do.

ii. "He doth not say, faith is dead without works, lest it should be thought that works were the cause of the life of faith; but *faith without works is dead*; implying, that works are the effects and signs of the life of faith." (Poole)

iii. What are some marks of saving faith?

- It is faith that looks not to self, but to Jesus Christ.
- It is faith that agrees with God's word, both inwardly and with words.
- It is faith that in itself is not a work that deserves reward from God; in this sense it is simply *refusing* to think God is a liar, and that in itself is not a good work, simply the absence of a sinful work.
- It is faith grounded in what Jesus did on the cross and by the empty tomb.
- It is faith that will *naturally* be expressed in repentance and good works.
- It is faith that may sometimes doubt; yet the doubts are not *bigger* than the faith nor are they *more permanent* than the faith. This faith can say, "Lord I believe; help my unbelief."
- It is faith that wants others to come to the same faith.
- It is faith that says *more* than "Lord, Lord" as in Matthew 7:21-23.
- It is faith that not only *hears* the word of God but *does* it, as in Matthew 7:24-27.

3. (18-19) A living faith cannot be separated from works.

But someone will say, "You have faith, and I have works." Show me your faith without your works, and I will show you my faith by my

works. You believe that there is one God. You do well. Even the demons believe; and tremble!

a. **You have faith, and I have works**: Some might try to say that some have the "gift" of **works** and others have the "gift" of **faith**. "It's fine for you to have your gift of **works** and that you care for the needy. But that isn't my gift." James will not allow this kind of thinking. Real faith will be demonstrated by works.

b. **Show me your faith without your works, and I will show you my faith by my works**: The appeal of James is clear and logical. We can't "see" someone's faith, but we *can* see their works. You can't see faith **without** works, but you can demonstrate the reality of faith **by** works.

c. **You believe that there is one God. You do well. Even the demons believe; and tremble!** The fallacy of faith without works is demonstrated by the **demons**, which have a "dead" faith in God. The demons **believe** in the sense that they acknowledge that God exists. But this kind of faith does nothing for the **demons**, because it isn't real faith, and that is proved by the fact that it doesn't have works along with it.

4. (20-24) Abraham as an example of living faith.

But do you want to know, O foolish man, that faith without works is dead? Was not Abraham our father justified by works when he offered Isaac his son on the altar? Do you see that faith was working together with his works, and by works faith was made perfect? And the Scripture was fulfilled which says, "Abraham believed God, and it was accounted to him for righteousness." And he was called the friend of God. You see then that a man is justified by works, and not by faith only.

a. **Do you want to know, O foolish man, that faith without works is dead?** James will now use the Old Testament to demonstrate what he has already said about the character of a living faith, showing that a **faith** that is not accompanied with **works** is a **dead** faith that cannon save.

b. **Was not Abraham our father justified by works when he offered Isaac his son on the altar?** Abraham was justified by faith long before he offered Isaac (Genesis 15:6). But his obedience in offering Isaac *demonstrated* that he really did trust God.

i. James properly estimates that Abraham actually *did* offer **Isaac his son on the altar**, even though the angel stopped him from actually killing his son. Yet he had **offered Isaac his son** in his firm resolution and intentions, and would have surely completed the act had not God stopped him. Abraham was so complete in his obedience that he counted Isaac as dead and set him **on the altar**.

c. **Faith was working together with his works, and by works faith was made perfect**: Faith and works cooperated perfectly together in Abraham. If he never had believed God, he could have never done the good work of obedience when asked to offer Isaac. As well, his faith was proven true – was completed, **was made perfect** – by his obedient works.

i. "Here is a proof that faith cannot exist without being active in works of righteousness. His faith in God would have been of no avail to him, had it not been manifested by works." (Clarke)

d. **You see then that a man is justified by works, and not by faith only**: The **faith only** that will not justify a man is a faith that is without works, a dead faith. But true faith, living faith, shown to be true by good works, will alone justify.

i. "It is faith that justifieth the man; but they are works that justify faith to be right and real, saving and justifying." (Trapp)

ii. Works *must* accompany a genuine faith, because genuine faith is always connected with regeneration - being born again, becoming a *new creation* in Jesus (2 Corinthians 5:17). If there is no evidence of a new life, then there was no genuine, saving faith.

iii. As Charles Spurgeon is reported to have said: "The grace that does not change my life will not save my soul."

5. (25-26) Rahab as an example of living faith.

Likewise, was not Rahab the harlot also justified by works when she received the messengers and sent *them* out another way? For as the body without the spirit is dead, so faith without works is dead also.

a. **Rahab the harlot**: Significantly, James used two examples of a living faith – Abrhaham (the father of the Jews) and Rahab (a Gentile). James perhaps is subtly rebuking the partiality that may have developed on the part of Jewish Christians against the Gentile believers starting to come into the church.

b. **Was not Rahab the harlot also justified by works**: Rahab demonstrated her trust in the God of Israel by hiding the spies and seeking salvation from their God (Joshua 2:8-13). Her faith was shown to be living faith because it *did* something. Her belief in the God of Israel would not have saved her if she had not *done* something with that faith.

i. The lesson from Abraham is clear: if we believe in God, we will do what He tells us to do. The lesson from Rahab is also clear: if we believe in God, we will help His people, even when it costs us something.

ii. "He designedly put together two persons so different in their character, in order more clearly to shew, that no one, whatever may have been his or her condition, nation, or class in society, has ever been counted righteous without good works." (Calvin, cited in Hiebert)

c. **For as the body without the spirit is dead, so faith without works is dead also**: As much as you can have a body with no life (a corpse), so you can have a faith with no life - and faith without works is a **dead** faith, unable to save.

> i. "Therefore, if no deeds are forthcoming, it is proof that the professed faith is dead. Notice that James does not deny that it is faith. He simply indicates that it is not the right kind of faith. It is not living faith, nor can it save." (Burdick)

> ii. We can think of an apple tree; where is the life of the tree? It is in the root, and underneath the bark of the tree in the trunk. The life is not in the apples, the fruit that is displayed in season; but if the tree is alive *it will produce apples in season*.

> iii. "Man is not justified by faith alone, that is, by a bare and empty knowledge of God; he is justified by works, that is, his righteousness is known and proved by its fruits." (Calvin)

James 3 – Warnings and Words to Teachers

A. The demonstration of a living faith in controlling what we say.

1. (1-2) Opening observations: the greater accountability of teachers and the difficulty of not stumbling.

My brethren, let not many of you become teachers, knowing that we shall receive a stricter judgment. For we all stumble in many things. If anyone does not stumble in word, he *is* a perfect man, able also to bridle the whole body.

a. **Let not many of you become teachers**: James has a sober admonition for those who would **become teachers** in the church. They must take the responsibility seriously, because their accountability is greater and they shall **receive a stricter judgment**.

i. It is easy to take the position of teacher lightly in the church, without considering its cost in terms of accountability. Jesus warned *to whom much is given, from him much will be required; and to whom much have been committed, of him they will ask the more.* (Luke 12:48)

ii. The words of Jesus and James remind us that being among the **teachers** in God's church is more than a matter of having natural or even spiritual gifts; there is an additional dimension of appropriate character and right living. "James found that this department of church-work had become extremely popular. Hence his warning about its serious responsibilities. God will judge us on the last day **with special strictness** on account of our influence over others." (Moffatt)

iii. Therefore, **teachers** were both tested more and would be judged more strictly. "Their case is awful; *they shall receive greater condemnation* than common sinners; they have not only sinned in thrusting themselves into that office to which God has never called them, but through their *insufficiency* the flocks over whom they have assumed the *mastery* perish for lack of knowledge, and their blood will God require at the watchman's hand." (Clarke)

iv. "The comparative adjective *greater* [**stricter**] implies degrees of treatment at the judgment seat." (Hiebert)

b. **For we all stumble in many things**: The greater accountability of teachers is especially sobering in light of our common weaknesses. After all, **we all stumble in many things**. The ancient Greek word translated **stumble** does not imply a fatal fall, but something that trips us up and hinders our spiritual progress.

i. **We all stumble**: James included himself among those who **stumble**. Yet he did not excuse his or our stumbling. We know that **we all stumble**, but we should all press on to a better walk with the Lord, marked by *less* stumbling.

ii. This is another of the several statements in the Bible which tell us that all men sin (also including 1 Kings 8:46; Job 14:4; Proverbs 20:9; Ecclesiastes 7:20; and 1 John 1:8, 10).

c. **If anyone does not stumble in word, he is a perfect man**: James provided a way to measure spiritual maturity for teachers and for all Christians. Jesus demonstrated in Matthew 12:34-37 that words are the revelation of the inner character.

i. To **not stumble in word** shows true spiritual maturity. This is especially relevant to teachers, who have so much more opportunity to sin with their tongue.

- We **stumble in word** about ourselves, with our boasting, exaggeration, and selective reporting.

- We **stumble in word** about others, with our criticism, gossip, slander, cruelty, two-facedness, and anger; or with flattery and insincere words meant to gain favor.

2. (3-6) The power of the tongue.

Indeed, we put bits in horses' mouths that they may obey us, and we turn their whole body. Look also at ships: although they are so large and are driven by fierce winds, they are turned by a very small rudder wherever the pilot desires. Even so the tongue is a little member and boasts great things. See how great a forest a little fire kindles! And the tongue *is* a fire, a world of iniquity. The tongue is so set among our members that it defiles the whole body, and sets on fire the course of nature; and it is set on fire by hell.

a. **We put bits in horses' mouths that they may obey us**: A small bit in the mouth controls a strong horse. A small rudder turns a large ship. Even so, if we have control over our tongue it is an indication that we have control over our self. Whoever can control the tongue can *bridle the whole body* (James 3:2).

i. The bit and the rudder are small but extremely important. If they are not controlled the entire horse is out of control and the entire ship is out of control. It is possible for something as small as the tongue is to have tremendous power for either good or evil.

ii. You don't solve the problem of an unruly horse by keeping it in the barn, or the problem of a hard-to-steer ship by keeping it tied to the dock. In the same way, even a vow of silence is not the ultimate answer for the misuse of our tongue.

iii. If the tongue is like a bit in the mouth of a horse or the rudder on a ship, it leaves us with the question: *Who or what holds the reigns, or who or what directs the rudder?* Some people have *no* hand on the reigns or rudder, and therefore say whatever comes into mind. Others direct their tongue from their emotions or from aspects of their carnal nature. James points us towards having the Spirit of God, working through the new man, set directing hands on the reigns and rudder that is our tongue.

b. **See how great a forest a little fire kindles! And the tongue is a fire, a world of iniquity**: The fire of the tongue has been used to burn many. Children are told *sticks and stones may break my bones, but words can never hurt me.* But that child's rhyme isn't really true; the bitter pain of a word spoken against us can hurt us for a lifetime, long after a broken bone has healed.

i. "In the two former illustrations, animals and ships are controlled by small objects; in this last illustration, a huge forest is destroyed by a tiny spark. The tongue likewise can either control or destroy." (Burdick)

ii. What others say to us and what we say to others can last a long time, for good or for evil. The casual sarcastic or critical remark can inflict a lasting injury on another person. The well-timed encouragement or compliment can inspire someone for the rest of their life.

iii. Proverbs speaks of the person who doesn't consider the destructive power of his words. *Like a madman who throws firebrands, arrows, and death, is the man who deceives his neighbor, and says, "I was only joking!"* (Proverbs 26:18-19).

iv. Again, James isn't telling us to never speak or to take a vow of silence; in many ways that would be *easier* than exercising true self-control over the tongue. The bridle, the rudder, and the fire can all do tremendous *good* when they are controlled properly.

c. **The tongue is a fire, a world of iniquity**: There aren't many sins that don't involve talking in some way. "It is though all the wickedness in the whole world were wrapped up in that little piece of flesh." (Burdick)

i. "It walketh through the earth, and faceth the very heavens, Psalm 73:9. It can run the world over and bite at everybody; being as a sharp razor . . . that instead of shaving the hair cutteth the throat, Psalm 52:2. It is made in the shape of sword; and David felt it as a sword in his bones, Psalm 42:10. It is thin, broad, and long, as an instrument most fit to empty both speaker's and the hearer's heart. It is of a flame-colour, as apt to set on fire the whole wheel of nature, James 3:6." (Trapp)

ii. James echoes the testimony of Proverbs regarding the tongue:

In the multitude of words sin is not lacking, but he who restrains his lips is wise. The tongue of the righteous is choice silver; the heart of the wicked is worth little. The lips of the righteous feed many, but fools die for lack of wisdom. (Proverbs 10:19-21)

Anxiety in the heart of man causes depression, but a good word makes it glad. (Proverbs 12:25)

Pleasant words are like a honeycomb, sweetness to the soul and health to the bones. (Proverbs 16:24)

Death and life are in the power of the tongue, and those who love it will eat its fruit. (Proverbs 18:21)

3. (7-8) The difficulty of taming the tongue.

For every kind of beast and bird, of reptile and creature of the sea, is tamed and has been tamed by mankind. But no man can tame the tongue. *It is* an unruly evil, full of deadly poison.

a. **Every kind of beast and bird . . . has been tamed by mankind**: A wild animal can be more easily tamed than the tongue. In fact, James tells us that **no man can tame the tongue**.

i. The human spirit has incredible capacity for sacrifice and self-control. Sometimes we hear a desperate survival story of someone who cuts off their own leg to get free from a tree that has fallen on them, and then they make it to a hospital for medical treatment. Yet that same man can't **tame the tongue** perfectly.

b. **No man can tame the tongue**: Nevertheless the **tongue** can be brought under the power and the control of the Holy Spirit. We might say that only God Himself is mightier than the human tongue!

c. **It is an unruly evil, full of deadly poison**: The untamable tongue is even more dangerous when we consider the **deadly poison** it can deliver.

i. "The poison of the tongue is no less deadly, it murders men's reputations by the slanders it utters, their souls by the lusts and passions it stirs up in them, and many times their bodies too by the contentions and quarrels it raiseth against men." (Poole)

ii. A woman once came to John Wesley and said she knew what her talent was and she said, "I think my talent from God is to speak my mind." Wesley replied, "I don't think God would mind if you buried that talent." Speaking forth everything that comes to mind is unwise, poisonous speech.

4. (9-12) The contradictory character of the tongue.

With it we bless our God and Father, and with it we curse men, who have been made in the similitude of God. Out of the same mouth proceed blessing and cursing. My brethren, these things ought not to be so. Does a spring send forth fresh *water* and bitter from the same opening? Can a fig tree, my brethren, bear olives, or a grapevine bear figs? Thus no spring yields both salt water and fresh.

a. **With it we bless our God and Father, and with it we curse men**: The tongue can be used for the highest calling (to **bless our God**) and it can be used for the lowest evil (to **curse men**). In those who are born again, it shouldn't be said that **out of the same mouth proceed blessing and cursing**.

i. Peter's tongue confessed Jesus as the Messiah, the Son of the living God *and* denied Jesus with curses. John said, "Little children, love one another" *and* he wanted to say the word to bring down fire from heaven upon a Samaritan village.

b. **These things ought not to be so**: Our speech should be consistently glorifying to God. We shouldn't use one vocabulary or one tone of speaking at church and a different one at home or on the job. Like a spring of water, our mouths shouldn't **send forth fresh . . . and bitter from the same opening**.

i. "This outburst of James suggests that he had suffered from the strife of tongues in the religious world . . . it reads like a transcript of bitter experience." (Moffatt)

c. **Thus no spring yields both salt water and fresh**: James points to the ultimate *impossibility* of such a contradiction. If bad fruit and bitter water continue to come forth, it means that there is no contradiction. The tree is bad and the spring is bad.

i. Jesus taught in Matthew 12:34-37 that a man's words are a reliable revelation of his inner character. What we say can indicate what we are.

ii. **Can a fig tree, my brethren, bear olives**: "It would be a monstrosity, a thing to be wondered at, and stared at as unnatural and absurd if a fig tree started bearing olive berries and *it is just as unnatural for a Christian to live in sin*. Can he so live as to bear the fruits of iniquity instead of the fruits of righteousness? God forbid that it should be so!" (Spurgeon)

iii. "Unless you are regenerated, born from above by a new and heavenly birth, you are not Christians, whatever you may be called, and you cannot, produce the fruit which is acceptable to God any more than a fig tree can produce olive berries." (Spurgeon)

- You can label a fig tree "Olive Tree" and that will not make it an olive tree.

- You can trim a fig tree to look like an olive tree, and that will not make it an olive tree.

- You can treat a fig tree like an olive tree, and that will not make it an olive tree.

- You can surround a fig tree with many olive trees, and that will not make it an olive tree.

- You can transplant that fig tree to the Mount of Olives, and that would not make it an olive tree.

B. The demonstration of a living faith in the presence of wisdom.

1. (13) Wisdom shows us how to do good works

Who *is* wise and understanding among you? Let him show by good conduct *that* his works *are done* in the meekness of wisdom.

a. **Who is wise and understanding among you?** At the beginning of James 3, the author addressed those who were teachers or wanted to be teachers among Christians. There he told such teachers how they should *talk*; here he speaks about how they should *live*.

i. "James addresses the person who is 'wise and understanding.' The word *sophos* ('wise') was the technical term among the Jews for the teacher, the scribe, the rabbi. It appears that the author is still speaking to those who would be teachers (cf. James 3:1); here it is not what they say that he is concerned with, but rather how they live." (Burdick)

b. **Who is wise . . . Let him show by good conduct**: Wisdom is not mere head knowledge. Real wisdom and **understanding** will show in our lives, by our **good conduct**.

i. In this sense wisdom and understanding are like faith; they are invisible, inner qualities. If a person considers himself to be **wise** or **understanding**, it is fair to expect that this invisible inner quality would show itself in regular life. Here James told us how to judge if a person really is **wise and understanding**.

c. **His works are done in the meekness of wisdom**: True **wisdom** is also evident by its meek manner. Those who do their good works in a way designed to bring attention to themselves show they lack true wisdom.

> i. On **meekness**: "*Prautes* is gentleness, but not a passive gentleness growing out of weakness or resignation. It is an active attitude of deliberate acceptance." (Burdick)

2. (14-16) The character of earthly wisdom.

But if you have bitter envy and self-seeking in your hearts, do not boast and lie against the truth. This wisdom does not descend from above, but *is* earthly, sensual, demonic. For where envy and self-seeking *exist*, confusion and every evil thing *are* there.

a. **Bitter envy and self-seeking**: These are the opposite of *the meekness of wisdom* mentioned in James 3:13. These words actually refer to someone who has a critical, contentious, fight-provoking manner.

> i. "It is out of keeping with the temper of **bitter jealousy and rivalry** (i.e. party-spirit, selfish ambition, factiousness). **Do not pride yourselves on that,** on the intensity and harsh zeal which lead to such unscrupulous partisanship, which are sometimes justified as loyalty **to the truth**." (Moffatt)

> ii. "Religious people my be extremely provoking, and defeat their own ends by overbearing methods; right views and sound counsels may lose their effect if they are expressed by men who are self-seeking partisans or unscrupulous controversialists." (Moffatt)

b. **Do not boast and lie against the truth**: Anyone who shows **bitter envy and self-seeking** should not deceive anyone - especially themselves - about how wise they are. They show a **wisdom** that is **earthly, sensual,** and **demonic**. Their wisdom is more characteristic of the world, the flesh, and the devil than of God.

> i. "**This wisdom**" that James referred to was not really wisdom at all. "It is the wisdom claimed by the would-be teachers of James 3:14 whose lives contradict their claims. Such 'wisdom' evaluates everything by worldly standards and makes personal gain life's highest goal." (Burdick)

> ii. **Earthly, sensual, demonic**: Adam Clarke defined each term:
> - **Earthly**: "Having this life only in view."
> - **Sensual**: "Animal-having for its object the gratification of the passions and animal propensities."
> - **Demonic**: "Demoniacal-inspired by demons, and maintained in the soul by their indwelling influence."

c. **Confusion and every evil thing**: This is the fruit of human, earthly wisdom. The wisdom of the world, the flesh, and the devil may be able to accomplish things, but always with the ultimate fruit of **confusion and every evil thing**.

3. (17-18) The character of heavenly wisdom.

But the wisdom that is from above is first pure, then peaceable, gentle, willing to yield, full of mercy and good fruits, without partiality and without hypocrisy. Now the fruit of righteousness is sown in peace by those who make peace.

a. **But the wisdom that is from above**: God's wisdom also has fruit. James here defined exactly what he meant by *the meekness of wisdom* in James 3:13.

b. **First pure, then peaceable, gentle, willing to yield, full of mercy and good fruits, without partiality and without hypocrisy**: The character of this wisdom is wonderful. It is full of love and a giving heart, consistent with the holiness of God.

i. This wisdom is **first pure**: "The reference is not to sexual purity but to the absence of any sinful attitude or motive." (Burdick)

ii. This wisdom is **then peaceable**: "This is one of the great words of character description in the NT. In the LXX it is used mostly of God's disposition as a King. He is gentle and kind, although in reality he has every reason to be stern and punitive toward men in their sin." (Burdick)

iii. This wisdom is **gentle**: "The man who is *epieikes* is the man who knows when it is actually wrong to apply the strict letter of the law. He knows how to forgive when strict justice gives him a perfect right to condemn. . . . It is impossible to find an English word to translate this quality. Matthew Arnold called it 'sweet reasonableness' and it is the ability to extend to others the kindly consideration we would wish to receive ourselves." (Barclay)

iv. This wisdom is **willing to yield**: "Not stubborn nor obstinate; of a yielding disposition in all indifferent things; obsequious, docile." (Clarke) "**Conciliatory** (only here in N.T.) is the opposite of stiff and unbending." (Moffatt) "*Eupeithes* can mean *easy to persuade*, not in the sense of being pliable and weak, but in the sense of not being stubborn and of being willing to listen to reason and to appeal. . . . true wisdom is not rigid but is willing to listen and skilled in knowing when wisely to yield." (Barclay)

v. This wisdom is **full of mercy**: It does not judge others strictly on the basis of the law, but will extend a generous hand **full of mercy**. This wisdom knows that the same measure of mercy we grant to others is the same measure God will use with us (Matthew 7:2).

vi. This wisdom is **full of . . . good fruits**: This wisdom can *be seen by the fruit it produces*. It isn't just the inner power to think and talk about things the right way; it is **full of . . . good fruits**.

vii. This wisdom is **without partiality**: "*Without partiality*; or, without judging, i.e. either a curious inquiring into the faults of others, to find matter for censures." (Poole)

viii. This wisdom is **without hypocrisy**: "Without *pretending to be what it is not*; acting always in *its own character*; never *working under a mask*. Seeking nothing but God's glory, and using no other means to attain it than those of his own prescribing." (Clarke)

ix. "These last two words [**without partiality** and **without hypocrisy**] rule out the habit of using speech to half reveal and half conceal the mind of the speaker, who has something (as we say) at the back of his mind all the time." (Moffatt)

c. **Now the fruit of righteousness is sown in peace**: This fruit is like a seed that will bear fruit as it is sown by **those who make peace**.

i. "*The fruit of righteousness*; either the fruit we bring forth, which is righteousness itself, Luke 3:8, 9; Romans 6:22; Philippians 1:11; or the fruit we reap, which is the reward of righteousness, viz. eternal life." (Poole)

ii. "Far from being theoretical and speculative, James's concept of wisdom is thoroughly practical. It is the understanding and attitude that result in true piety and godliness." (Burdick)

James 4 - The Humble Dependence of a True Faith

A. The humble character of a living faith.

    1. (1-3) Reasons for strife in the Christian community.

Where do wars and fights *come* from among you? Do *they* not *come* from your *desires for* pleasure that war in your members? You lust and do not have. You murder and covet and cannot obtain. You fight and war. Yet you do not have because you do not ask. You ask and do not receive, because you ask amiss, that you may spend *it* on your pleasures.

    a. **Where do wars and fights come from among you?** James accurately described strife among Christians with the terms **wars and fights**. Often the battles that happen among Christians are bitter and severe.

        i. "He does not mean that they war within a man – although that is also true – but that they set men warring against each other." (Barclay)

    b. **Do they not come from your desires for pleasure that war in your members?** The source of **wars and fights** among Christians is always the same. There is some root of carnality, an internal **war** within the believer regarding the lusts of the flesh. No two believers who are both walking in the Spirit of God towards each other can live with **wars and fights** among themselves.

        i. "James seems to be bothered more by the selfish spirit and bitterness of the quarrels than by the rights and wrongs of the various viewpoints." (Moo)

        ii. Almost all who have such a critical and contentious attitude claim they are prompted and supported by the Spirit of God. James makes it clear that this contentious manner comes **from your desires**. "It is self-evident that the Spirit of God does not create desire which issues in envying." (Morgan)

    c. **Your desires for pleasure that war in your members**: The types of **desires** that lead to conflict are described. *Covetousness* leads to conflict (**you**

lust and do not have). *Anger* and *animosity* lead to hatred and conflict (**murder**).

> i. Again James looked back to the Sermon on the Mount when Jesus also used **murder** to express more than actual killing, but also as an inward condition of heart, shown outwardly by anger (Matthew 5:21-22).

> ii. "The word *kill* [**murder**] is startling and meant to startle; James sought to force his readers to realize the depth of the evil in their bitter hatred toward others." (Hiebert)

d. **Yet you do not have**: This points to the *futility* of this life lived for the **desires for pleasure**. Not only is it a life of conflict, but it is also a fundamentally *unsatisfied* life.

> i. "The whole history of mankind shows the failure of evil lustings to obtain their object." (Spurgeon)

> ii. This is the tragic irony of the life lived after worldly and fleshly desires; it never reaches the goal it gives everything for. This fundamental dissatisfaction is not because of a lack of effort: "If the lusters fail, it is not because they did not set to work to gain their ends; for according to their nature they used the most practical means within their reach, and used them eagerly, too." (Spurgeon)

> iii. This helps us to rationally understand the folly of living life after the lusts of the world and our animal appetites. You are tempted to fulfill a sinful desire because you think (or hope) that it may be *satisfied*, but it will *never* be satisfied. Why not accept your lack of such satisfaction now, instead of after much painful and harmful sin?

e. **Yet you do not have because you do not ask**: The reason these destructive desires exist among Christians is because they do not seek God for their needs (**you do not ask**). James reminds us here of the great power of prayer, and why one may live unnecessarily as a spiritual pauper, simply because they do not pray, or do not **ask** when they pray.

> i. We might state it as a virtual spiritual law: that God does not give unless we ask. If we possess little of God and His Kingdom, almost certainly we have asked little. "Remember this text: Jehovah says to his own Son, 'Ask of me and I will give thee the heathen for thine inheritance, and the uttermost parts of the earth for thy possession.' If the royal and divine Son of God cannot be exempted from the rule of asking that he may have, you and I cannot expect the rule to be relaxed in our favor. Why should it be?" (Spurgeon)

> ii. "If you may have everything by asking, and nothing without asking, I beg you to see how absolutely vital prayer is, and I beseech you to abound in it. . . . Do you know, brothers, what great things are to be

had for the asking? Have you ever thought of it? Does it not stimulate you to pray fervently? All heaven lies before the grasp of the asking man; all the promises of God are rich and inexhaustible, and their fulfillment is to be had by prayer." (Spurgeon)

f. **You ask amiss, that you may spend it on your pleasures**: After dealing with the problem of *no prayer*, now James addressed the problem of *selfish prayer*. These ones, when they did ask, they asked God with purely selfish motives.

> i. We must remember that the purpose of prayer is not to persuade a reluctant God to do our bidding. The purpose of prayer is to align our will with His, and in partnership with Him, to ask Him to accomplish His will on this earth (Matthew 6:10).

> ii. "When a man so prays he asks God to be his servant, and gratify his desires; nay, worse than that, he wants God to join him in the service of his lusts. He will gratify his lusts, and God shall come and help him to do it. Such prayer is blasphemous, but a large quantity of it is offered, and it must be one of the most God-provoking things that heaven ever beholds." (Spurgeon)

> iii. **Spend** is the same verb used to describe the wasteful spending of the Prodigal Son in Luke 15:14. Destructive desires persist, even if we pray, because our prayers may be self-centered and self-indulgent.

2. (4-5) A rebuke of compromise and covetousness among Christians.

Adulterers and adulteresses! Do you not know that friendship with the world is enmity with God? Whoever therefore wants to be a friend of the world makes himself an enemy of God. Or do you think that the Scripture says in vain, "The Spirit who dwells in us yearns jealously"?

a. **Adulterers and adulteresses**: This is a rebuke presented in Old Testament vocabulary. God spoke this way in the Old Testament when His people were attracted to some form of idolatry (Jeremiah 3:8-9, Ezekiel 6:9, Ezekiel 16:32, Ezekiel 23:37, and Hosea 3:1). As James saw it here, their covetousness was idolatry (Colossians 3:5) and **friendship with the world**.

> i. Better ancient Greek manuscripts only say *you adulteresses*. "He uses the feminine form deliberately, for one turn of special contempt and scorn in the ancient world was to call a community or group by some feminine equivalent." (Moffatt)

> ii. The addition of **adulterers** was probably from an early scribe who thought James meant literal sexual adultery and didn't want to exclude men from the rebuke. But James used the phrase *you adulteresses* to give a specific spiritual picture. According to this picture, God is the "husband" and we are His "wife" (as in Old Testament passages such as Isaiah 54:5, Jeremiah 3:20, and Exodus 34:15-16).

iii. "The Jews, because of their *covenant* with God, are represented as being *espoused* to him; and hence, their idolatry, and their iniquity in general, are represented under the notion of *adultery*." (Clarke)

iv. "You have your hearts full of harlotry . . . this vile strumpet the world, that lays forth her two breasts of profit and pleasure, and ensnareth many; for the which she must be burnt, as a whore, by the fire of the last day." (Trapp)

b. **Do you not know that friendship with the world is enmity with God?** James recognizes that we cannot both be friends of this world system in rebellion against God, and friends of God at the same time (Matthew 6:24). Even the *desire* to be a friend (**wants to be a friend**) of the world makes that one an **enemy of God**.

i. "Such **friendship with the world** means that one is on a footing of hostility towards God, for it defies His will and despises His purpose; disguise it as one may, it is an implicit challenge to God." (Moffatt)

ii. The strong statements James made here remind us that all was not beautiful in the early church. They had plenty of carnality and worldliness to deal with. While the New Testament church is a clear pattern for us, we should not over-romanticize the spiritual character of early Christians.

c. **The Spirit who dwells in us yearns jealously**: The indwelling presence of the Holy **Spirit** has a jealous yearning for our friendship with God. The **Spirit** will convict the Christian who lives in compromise.

i. This phrase is a little hard to accurately translate. Is it *God jealously yearning for the devotion of our spirit which He put within us*, or is it the *Spirit within us jealously yearning for the full devotion of our heart*? Either way, the sense is much the same.

ii. "He went so far as to speak of them as adulterers and adulteresses; and then adopting a gentler, pleading tone, he says, 'You are grieving the Holy Spirit who has come to dwell within you, who yearns with a jealous envy to possess your entire nature for Himself.'" (Meyer)

iii. James agrees with the many passages in the Old Testament that tell us God is a jealous God (Deuteronomy 32:16 and 32:21; Exodus 20:5 and 34:14; Zechariah 8:2). "The idea is that God loves men with such a passion that he cannot bear any other love within the hearts of men." (Barclay)

iv. Think of the inner pain and torture inside the person who is betrayed by an unfaithful spouse; who must reckon with the truth, *I am faithful to them, but they are not faithful to me*. This is what the Spirit of God feels regarding our world-loving hearts.

d. **The Scripture says**: One cannot find this exact quote ("**The Spirit who dwells in us yearns jealously**") in any specific Old Testament verse. James seemed to present an idea that is alluded to in several passages without quoting any specific passage.

> i. "More probably is the view that James was not citing a particular passage but summarizing the truth expressed in several Old Testament passages." (Hiebert)

> ii. Or it may be that James 4:5 speaks in two independent sentences, and that the words of **Scripture** quoted refer to what was said in James 4:4.

3. (6-10) The solutions for strife: in humility, get right with God.

But He gives more grace. Therefore He says: "God resists the proud, But gives grace to the humble." Therefore submit to God. Resist the devil and he will flee from you. Draw near to God and He will draw near to you. Cleanse *your* hands, *you* sinners; and purify *your* hearts, *you* double-minded. Lament and mourn and weep! Let your laughter be turned to mourning and *your* joy to gloom. Humble yourselves in the sight of the Lord, and He will lift you up.

a. **But He gives more grace**: The same Holy Spirit convicting us of our compromise will also grant us the **grace** to serve God as we should. This wonderful statement – **but He gives more grace** – stands in strong contrast to the previous words.

> i. "Note that contrast; note it always. Observe how weak we are, how strong he is; how proud we are, how condescending he is; how erring we are, and how infallible he is; how changing we are, and how immutable he is; how provoking we are, and how forgiving he is. Observe how in us there is only ill, and how in him there is only good. Yet our ill but draws his goodness forth, and still he blesseth. Oh! What a rich contrast!" (Spurgeon)

> ii. "Sin seeks to enter, grace shuts the door; sin tries to get the mastery, but grace, which is stronger than sin, resists, and will not permit it. Sin gets us down at times, and puts its foot on our neck; grace comes to the rescue . . . Sin comes up like Noah's flood, but grace rides over the tops of the mountains like the ark." (Spurgeon)

> iii. "Do you suffer from spiritual poverty? It is your own fault, for he giveth more grace. If you have not got it, it is not because it is not to be had, but because you have not gone for it." (Spurgeon)

b. **God resists the proud**: At the same time, James reminds us that this **grace** only comes **to the humble**. Grace and pride are eternal enemies. Pride demands that God bless me in light of my merits, whether real or imagined. But grace will not deal with me on the basis of anything in me – good or bad – but only on the basis of who God is.

    i. James used a powerful word in the phrase, **resists the proud**: "*Sets himself in battle array* against him." (Clarke) "*God resisteth the proud*, 'setteth himself in battle-array against such,' above all other sorts of sinner, as invaders of his territories, and foragers or plunderers of his chief treasures." (Trapp)

c. **But gives grace to the humble**: It isn't as if our humility *earns* the grace of God. Humility merely puts us in a position to receive the gift He freely **gives**.

d. **Therefore submit to God**: In light of the grace offered to the humble, there is only one thing to do: **submit to God**. This means to order yourself under God, to surrender to Him as a conquering King, and start receiving the benefits of His reign.

    i. It is a wonder that the world does not submit to God. "I have heard much of the rights of man: but it were well also to consider the rights of God, which are the first, highest, surest, and most solemn rights in the universe, and lie at the base of all other rights. . . . Alas, great God, how art thou a stranger even in the world which thou hast thyself made! Thy creatures, who could not see if thou hadst not given them eyes, look everywhere except to thee. Creatures who could not think if thou hadst not given them minds, think of all things except thee; and beings who could not live if thou didst not keep them in being, forget thee utterly, or if they remember thine existence, and see thy power, are foolhardy enough to become thy foes!" (Spurgeon)

    ii. "If he were a tyrant it might be courageous to resist, but since he is a Father it is ungrateful to rebel." (Spurgeon) Instead, Spurgeon (in another sermon) suggested reasons why we should **submit to God**:

- We should submit to God because He created us.
- We should submit to God because His rule is good for us.
- We should submit to God because all resistance to Him is futile.
- We should submit to God because such submission is absolutely necessary to salvation.
- We should submit to God because it is the only way to have peace with God.

    iii. "I desire to whisper one little truth in your ear, and I pray that it may startle you: *You are submitting even now*. You say, 'Not I; am lord of myself.' I know you think so, but all the while you are submitting to the devil. The verse before us hints at this. 'Submit yourselves unto God. Resist the devil, and he will flee from you.' If you do not submit to God you never will resist the devil, and you will remain constantly under his tyrannical power. Which shall be your master, God or devil, for one of these must? No man is without a master." (Spurgeon)

e. **Resist the devil and he will flee from you**: To solve the problems of carnality and the strife it causes, we must also **resist the devil**. This means to stand against devil's deceptions and his efforts to intimidate. As we **resist the devil**, we are *promised* that **he will flee from you**.

i. Significantly, James does not recommend that demons should be cast out of believers by a third party. Instead, James simply challenges individual Christians to deal with Satan as a conquered foe who can and must be personally resisted. "He who, in the *terrible name* of JE-SUS, opposes even the devil himself is sure to have speedy and glorious conquest. He flees from that *name*, and from his conquering blood." (Clarke)

ii. **Resist** comes from two Greek words: *stand* and *against*. James tells us to *stand against* the devil. Satan can be set running by the resistance of the lowliest believer who comes in the authority of what Jesus did on the cross.

iii. "*Resist*, by faith, and the rest of the spiritual armour, Ephesians 6:13, 14, etc. Or, *resist* i.e. comply not with his motions and temptations." (Poole)

iv. "*And he will flee from you*; as to that particular assault in which you resist him; and though he return again, and tempt you again, yet you still resisting, he will still be overcome; ye are never conquered so long as you do not consent." (Poole)

v. A famous ancient Christian writer named Hermas wrote, "The devil can wrestle against the Christian, but he cannot pin him." (Cited in Barclay)

f. **Draw near to God and He will draw near to you**: The call to **draw near to God** is both an invitation and a promise. It is no good to submit to God's authority and to resist the devil's attack and then fail to **draw near to God**. We have it as a promise: God **will draw near to** us as we draw near to Him.

i. "When a soul sets out to seek God, God sets out to meet that soul; so that while we are drawing near to him, he is drawing near to us." (Clarke)

ii. What does it mean to **draw near to God**? Spurgeon considered a few ways:

- It means to draw near in *worship, praise, and in prayer.*
- It means to draw near by *asking counsel of God.*
- It means to draw near in *enjoying communion with God.*
- It means to draw near in *the general course and tenor of your life.*

iii. In one way, this text illustrates the difference between the old covenant and the new covenant. In the old covenant, God told Moses to not come any closer to the burning bush and take off his shoes. Under the new covenant, God says to the sinner: "Draw near to Me and I will draw near to you." Now the ground between God and the sinner has been sprinkled with the blood of Jesus, and we can come close to God on the basis of that blood.

iv. This also shows *what God wants to do for the sinner.* It doesn't say, "Draw near to God and He will *save* you" or "Draw near to God and He will *forgive* you," though both of those are true. But what God really wants is to be *near* man; to have a close relationship and fellowship with the individual.

v. From the rest of the chapter we see the results of drawing near to God:

- Drawing near to God helps us to resist the devil.
- Drawing near to God helps us to become pure.
- Drawing near to God helps us to sorrow for sin.
- Drawing near to God helps us to speak well of other people.
- Drawing near to God helps us to think of eternal things.

g. **Cleanse your hands, you sinners; and purify your hearts, you double-minded. Lament and mourn and weep!** As we draw near to God, we will be convicted of our sin. So we **lament and mourn and weep** as appropriate under the conviction of sin, and we are compelled to find cleansing at the cross.

i. "The word used for sinner is *hamartolos*, which means the hardened sinner, the man whose sin is obvious and notorious." (Barclay)

ii. In using terms like **lament and mourn and weep**, "James speaks in terms of the Hebrew prophets' language about the anguish of repentance." (Moffatt)

h. **Humble yourselves in the sight of the Lord, and He will lift you up**: As we come as sinners before the holy God (not as self righteous religionists, as Jesus explained in Luke 18:10-14), we appropriately **humble** ourselves before Him. Then He will **lift** us **up**, because *God resists the proud, but gives grace to the humble*, and grace - the unmerited favor of God - always lifts us up.

i. In this passage James has powerfully described both the *duty* and the *blessing* of repentance.

4. (11-12) The solutions for strife: get right with other people.

Do not speak evil of one another, brethren. He who speaks evil of a brother and judges his brother, speaks evil of the law and judges the law. But if you judge the law, you are not a doer of the law but a judge. There is one Lawgiver, who is able to save and to destroy. Who are you to judge another?

a. **Do not speak evil of one another**: Humbling ourselves and getting right with God *must* result in our getting right with other people. When we are right with other people, it will show in the way we talk about them. So we must **not speak evil of one another** and not judge our brother.

i. **Speak evil** translates the ancient Greek word *katalalia*. "*Katalalia* is the sin of those who meet in corners and gather in little groups and pass on confidential information which destroy the good name of those who are not there to defend themselves." (Barclay)

ii. This sin is wrong for two reasons. First, it breaks the royal law that we should love one another. Second, it takes a right of judgment that only God has.

b. **He who speaks evil of a brother and judges his brother, speaks evil of the law and judges the law**: When we judge our brother, we put ourselves in the same place as the law, in effect judging the law. This is something that we have no authority to do, because **there is one Lawgiver** - so **who are you to judge another?**

i. "However high and orthodox our view of God's law might be, a failure actually to do it says to the world that we do not *in fact* put much store by it." (Moo)

c. **Who are you to judge another?** This is an extension of the same humility that James writes about in this chapter. When we have proper humility before God, it just isn't within us to arrogantly judge our brother.

i. "This is not to rule out civil courts and judges. Instead, it is to root out the harsh, unkind, critical spirit that continually finds fault with others." (Burdick)

ii. "*Who art thou*; what a sorry creature, a man, a worm, that thou shouldest lift up thyself into God's place, and make thyself a judge of one not subject to thee!" (Poole)

B. A humble dependence on God.

1. (13-16) A caution against an attitude of independence from God.

Come now, you who say, "Today or tomorrow we will go to such and such a city, spend a year there, buy and sell, and make a profit"; whereas you do not know what *will happen* tomorrow. For what *is* your life? It is even a vapor that appears for a little time and then vanishes away. Instead you *ought* to say, "If the Lord wills, we shall live and do this or that." But now you boast in your arrogance. All such boasting is evil.

a. **You who say, "Today or tomorrow we will go to such and such a city, spend a year there, buy and sell, and make a profit"**: James rebuked the kind of heart that lives and makes its plans apart from a constant awareness of the hand of God, and with an underestimation of our own limitations (**you do not know what will happen tomorrow**).

i. "This was the custom of those ancient times; they traded from city to city, carrying their goods on the backs of camels. The Jews traded thus to *Tyre, Sidon, Caesarea, Crete, Ephesus, Philippi, Thessalonica, Corinth, Rome*, &c. And it is to this kind of itinerant mercantile life that St. James alludes." (Clarke)

ii. This attitude that James challenged goes far beyond making wise plans for the future. "Not, let us go, but, *we will go*, in the indicative mood; noting the peremptoriness of their purposes, and their presuming upon future times and things, which were not in their power." (Poole)

iii. "Notice, that these people, while they thought everything was at their disposal, used everything for worldly objects. What did they say? Did they determine with each other 'We will to-day or to-morrow do such and such a thing for the glory of God, and for the extension of his kingdom'? Oh, no, there was not a word about God in it, from beginning to end!" (Spurgeon)

iv. "There are two great certainties about things that shall come to pass – one is that God knows, and the other is that we do not know." (Spurgeon)

b. **For what is your life? It is even a vapor that appears for a little time and then vanishes away**: James asked us to consider the fragility of human life, and the fact that we live and move only at the permission of God. James does not discourage us from planning and doing, only from planning and doing *apart from* reliance on God.

i. The idea that our life was a **vapor** or shadow was a frequent figure of speech in the Old Testament (Psalm 102:11; Job 8:9; 1 Chronicles 29:15).

ii. We also remember the story Jesus told about the rich man who made his great plans for the future, and foolishly lost it all when his soul was required of him (Luke 12:16-21). "They might easily observe that many things fall out betwixt the cup and the lip, betwixt the chin and the chalice." (Trapp)

iii. "There are a thousand gates to death; and, though some seem to be narrow wickets, many souls have passed through them. Men have been choked by a grape stone, killed by a tile falling from the roof of a house, poisoned by a drop, carried off by a whiff of foul air. I know not what there is that is too little to slay the greatest king. It is a marvel that man lives at all." (Spurgeon)

iv. Knowing that life is short, we must be diligent and energetic about the common duties of everyday life. "*It is sinful to neglect the common duties of life*, under the idea that we shall do something more by-and-by. You do not obey your parents, young man, and yet you are going to be a minister, are you? A pretty minister will you make! As an apprentice you are very dilatory and neglectful, and your master would be glad to see the back of you; he wishes that he could burn your indentures; and yet you have an idea you are going to be a missionary, I believe? A pretty missionary you would be!" (Spurgeon)

c. **Instead you ought to say, "If the Lord wills, we shall live and do this or that."** It is nothing but sheer **arrogance** that makes us think that we can live and move and have our being independent of God. This boastful **arrogance** is the essence of sin: a proud independence, the root of all sin, as was the case with Lucifer (Isaiah 14:12-15) and Adam (Genesis 3:5-7).

i. Paul knew and lived this principle: *I will return again to you, God willing* (Acts 18:21). *But I will come to you shortly, if the Lord wills* (1 Corinthians 4:19). *I hope to stay a while with you, if the Lord permits* (1 Corinthians 16:7).

ii. "**All such boasting**, when life is so precarious, is worse than absurd, it is **wicked**, a positive sin, a specimen of the ungodly haughtiness (James 4:6) of which men should repent." (Moffatt)

iii. **You boast in your arrogance**: "The word is *alazoneia. Alazoneia* was originally the characteristic of the wandering quack. He offered cures which were no cures and boasted to things that he was not able to do." (Moffatt)

2. (17) A challenge to live according to what we know in the Lord.

Therefore, to him who knows to do good and does not do *it*, to him it is sin.

a. **To him who knows to do good and does not do it, to him it is sin**: James knows that it is far easier to *think about* and *talk about* humility and dependence on God than it is to live it. Yet he makes the mind of God plain: as we know these things, we are accountable to *do them*.

i. Here James returned to his consistent theme through his letter: the idea that genuine faith is proved by action. "However high and orthodox our view of God's law might be, a failure actually to do it says to the world that we do not *in fact* put much store by it." (Moo)

ii. Yet we also see that the uncertainty of life, to which James referred to in the previous passage, should not create fear that makes one passive or inactive. The uncertainty of life should make us ready to recognize what is **good** and then **do it**. "This uncertainty of life is not a cause either for fear or inaction. It is always a reason for realizing our complete dependence on God." (Moffatt)

b. **To him it is sin**: Jesus told a story with much the same point in Luke 12:41-48. The story was about servants and how they obeyed the master in the master's absence. Jesus concluded the story with this application: *For everyone to whom much is given, from him much will be required; and to whom much has been committed, of him they will ask the more* (Luke 12:48). Greater light gives greater responsibility.

James 5 – The Life of a Living Faith

A. A rebuke of the ungodly rich.

1. (1-3) The rich and the illusion of wealth.

Come now, *you* rich, weep and howl for your miseries that are coming upon *you!* Your riches are corrupted, and your garments are moth-eaten. Your gold and silver are corroded, and their corrosion will be a witness against you and will eat your flesh like fire. You have heaped up treasure in the last days.

a. **Come now, you rich**: James had developed the idea of the need for complete dependence on God. He now naturally rebuked those most likely to live independently from God – the **rich**.

i. While Jesus counted some **rich** persons among His followers (such as Zaccheus, Joseph of Armithea, and Barnabas), we are compelled to observe that riches do present an additional and significant obstacle to the kingdom (Matthew 19:23-24). It is also true that the pursuit of riches is a motivation for every conceivable sin (1 Timothy 6:10).

ii. "He speaks to them not simply as rich (for riches and grace sometimes may go together) but as wicked, not only wallowing in wealth, but abusing it to pride, luxury, oppression, and cruelty." (Poole)

b. **Weep and howl**: In the style of an Old Testament prophet, James tells the rich to mourn in consideration of their destiny (the **miseries that are coming upon you**). In the life to come, their riches will be revealed as **corrupted**, **moth-eaten** and **corroded**.

i. James probably refers to the destruction of three kinds of wealth. Stores of food are **corrupted** (rotted), **garments are moth-eaten**, and **gold and silver are corroded**. Each one of them comes to nothing in their own way.

ii. "More than that, James adds, with a Dantesque touch of horror, **the rust will devour** (or corrode) **your flesh like fire**, you are so bound up with your greedy gains; your wealth perishes and you perish with it and by it, eaten away in burning pain." (Moffatt)

iii. "Better weep here, where there are wiping handkerchiefs in the hand of Christ, than to have your eyes whipped out in hell. Better howl with men than yell with devils." (Trapp)

c. **Will be a witness against you**: The corruptible nature of the wealth of the rich will **witness against** them. On the day of judgment it will be revealed that they have lived their lives in the arrogant independence James previously condemned, heaping up earthly **treasure in the last days**, when they should have been heaping up treasure in heaven (Luke 18:22).

i. **In the last days**: "The doom is depicted in highly coloured Jewish phrases, and the same immediate prospect of the End is held out as a threat to the rich and as a consolation to the oppressed poor." (Moffatt)

2. (4-6) The sins of the rich are condemned.

Indeed the wages of the laborers who mowed your fields, which you kept back by fraud, cry out; and the cries of the reapers have reached the ears of the Lord of Sabaoth. You have lived on the earth in pleasure and luxury; you have fattened your hearts as in a day of slaughter. You have condemned, you have murdered the just; he does not resist you.

a. **The wages of the laborers . . . you kept back by fraud**: They had withheld **the wages of** their **laborers**. They lived indulgently without regard for others (as the man in Jesus' story about the rich man and Lazarus, Luke 16:19-31). They had condemned and murdered from their position of power.

i. "Deferring payment is a sort of defrauding, as it bereaves the creditor of the benefit of improvement; and so they are taxed here with injustice, as well as covetousness, in that they lived upon other men's labours, and starved the poor to enrich themselves." (Poole)

b. **The cries of the reapers have reached the ears of the Lord of Sabaoth**: The title **Lord of Sabaoth** in James 5:4 should not be confused with the similar title *Lord of the Sabbath* (used in Mark 2:28 and Luke 6:5). Instead it is a translation of the idea behind the Hebrew term *Lord of Hosts* (compare Romans 9:29 with Isaiah 1:9), which means "the Lord of armies," especially in the sense of heavenly and angelic armies. It describes God as the warrior, the commander-in-chief of all heavenly armies.

i. The use of this title was meant to give these unjust reach a sober warning. The cries of the people they had oppressed had come to the ears of the God who commands heavenly armies; the God of might and power and judgment.

ii. "The primary reference is to Yahweh as the God of hosts or the armies of Israel and later the hosts of heaven. The rabbis rarely use the title, but Exodus 3:6 connects it with Yahweh's war against injustice." (Adamson)

iii. This is "a frequent appellation of God in the Old Testament; and signifies his uncontrollable power, and the infinitely numerous means he has for governing the world, and defending his followers, and punishing the wicked." (Clarke)

c. **You have condemned, you have murdered the just; he does not resist you**: Often those who are poor and without power in this world have little satisfaction from justice. Yet God hears their cries, and He is the one who guarantees to ultimately right every wrong and answer every injustice.

i. **Condemned . . . you have murdered the just**: "Take it either properly, or metaphorically of usurers and extortioners, that not only rob, but ravish the poor that are fallen into their nets." (Trapp)

B. A call for patient endurance in light of the coming judgment.

1. (7-8) Imitate the patient endurance of the farmer.

Therefore be patient, brethren, until the coming of the Lord. See *how* the farmer waits for the precious fruit of the earth, waiting patiently for it until it receives the early and latter rain. You also be patient. Establish your hearts, for the coming of the Lord is at hand.

a. **Therefore be patient, brethren**: James brought the issue of the ultimate judgment before us in his remarks about the ungodly rich and their destiny. Now he calls Christians (especially those enduring hardship) to patiently endure **until the coming of the Lord**.

i. "James stirs no class-feeling, e.g. of labourers against their unjust employers; leave the wealthy oppressors to God's imminent vengeance on their cruelty." (Moffatt)

ii. "Sometimes, indeed, the very hope of the coming of the Lord has seemed to increase impatience rather than patience. . . . Oh, to be patient in fellowship with God!" (Morgan)

b. **See how the farmer waits for the precious fruit of the earth, waiting patiently**: A farmer does not give up when his crop does not come to harvest immediately. He keeps on working even when the crop cannot be seen at all. Even so Christians must work hard and exercise patient endurance even when the harvest day seems far away.

i. As James instructs us, we are to wait upon God and not lose heart. "A man to whom it is given to wait for a reward keeps up his courage, and when he has to wait, he says, 'It is no more than I expected. I never reckoned that I was to slay my enemy at the first blow. I never imagined that I was to capture the city as soon as ever I had digged the first trench; I reckoned upon waiting, and now that is come, I find that God gives me the grace to fight on and wrestle on, till the victory shall come.' And patience saves a man from a great deal of haste and folly." (Spurgeon)

ii. When we think about it, the waiting and need for endurance we have in the Christian life is very much like the waiting of the farmer.

- He waits with a reasonable hope and expectation of reward.

- He waits a long time.

- He waits working all the while.

- He waits depending on things out of his own power; with his eye on the heavens.

- He waits despite changing circumstances and many uncertainties.

- He waits encouraged by the value of the harvest.

- He waits encouraged by the work and harvest of others.

- He waits because he really has no other option.

- He waits because it does no good to give up.

- He waits aware of how the seasons work.

- He waits because as time goes on, it becomes more important and not less to do so.

c. **Until it receives the early and latter rain**: The pictures of the **early and latter rain** should be taken literally as James intends. He refers to the early rains (coming in late October or early November) that were essential to soften the ground for plowing, and to the latter rains (coming in late April or May) which were essential to the maturing of the crops shortly before harvest. There is no allegorical picture *here* of an early and a latter outpouring of the Holy Spirit on the church.

i. The Bible does explain that there will be a significant outpouring of the Holy Spirit in the last days (Joel 2:28-29, Acts 2:17-18); but this passage from James doesn't seem to be relevant to that outpouring.

ii. Instead, the sense here is more as Moffatt explains: "The farmer had to wait for this rainfall twice in the year; but although he could do nothing to bring it, he did not lose heart, provided that he was obeying the will of his God."

d. **Establish your hearts, for the coming of the Lord is at hand**: The soon return of Jesus requires that we have *established* hearts, hearts that are rooted in Jesus and His eternal resolution of all things.

i. "When God shall give you a rich return for all you have done for him, you will blush to think you ever doubted; you will be ashamed to think you ever grew weary in his service. You shall have your reward. Not tomorrow, so wait: not the next day perhaps, so be patient. You may be full of doubts one day, your joys sink low. It may be rough windy weather with you in your spirit. You may even doubt whether you are the Lord's, but if you have rested in the name of Jesus, if by the grace of God you are what you are, if he is all your salvation, and all your desire, — have patience; have patience, for the reward will surely come in God's good time." (Spurgeon)

e. **For the coming of the Lord is at hand**: There is a real sense in which **the coming of the Lord** was **at hand** in the days of James as well as in our own day today. One might say that since the Ascension of Jesus, history has been brought to the brink of consummation and now runs parallel along side the edge of the brink, with the **coming of the Lord . . . at hand**.

2. (9) Practicing patient endurance among God's people.

Do not grumble against one another, brethren, lest you be condemned. Behold, the Judge is standing at the door!

a. **Do not grumble against one another**: Times of hardship can cause us to be less than loving with our Christian brothers and sisters. James reminds us that we cannot become grumblers and complainers in our hardship - lest we **be condemned** even in our hardship.

b. **Behold, the Judge is standing at the door!** Jesus comes as a **Judge**, not only to judge the world, but also to assess the faithfulness of Christians (2 Corinthians 5:10). In light of this, we cannot allow hardship to make us unloving towards each other.

3. (10-11) Following examples of patient endurance.

My brethren, take the prophets, who spoke in the name of the Lord, as an example of suffering and patience. Indeed we count them blessed who endure. You have heard of the perseverance of Job and seen the end *intended by* the Lord; that the Lord is very compassionate and merciful.

a. **Take the prophets . . . as an example of suffering and patience**: James reminds us that the prophets of the Old Testament endured hardship, yet practiced patient endurance. We can take them as examples.

i. Among these **prophets**, Jeremiah is one example of someone who endured mistreatment with patience. He was put in the stocks (Jeremiah 20:2), thrown into prison (Jeremiah 32:2), and lowered into miry dungeon (Jeremiah 28:6). Yet he persisted in his ministry.

ii. "As much as God honoured and loved them, yet they were not exempted from afflictions, but were maligned, traduced, and persecuted by men, 1 Kings 18:13; 19:14; 2 Kings 6:31; Amos 7:10; Hebrews 11; and therefore when they suffered such hard things, it is no shame for you to suffer the like, Matthew 5:12." (Poole)

b. **You have heard of the perseverance of Job**: James essentially tells us three things about Job and why he is a significant example for the suffering Christian.

i. First we see the **perseverance of Job**. Passages such as Job 1:20-22 show us the tremendous **perseverance** of this afflicted man, who refused to curse God despite his severe and mysterious suffering.

ii. We see also **the end intended by the Lord**, speaking of the ultimate goal and purpose of God in allowing the suffering to come upon Job. Perhaps the greatest **end intended by the Lord** was to use Job as a lesson to angelic beings, even as God promises to use the church (Ephesians 3:10-11).

- If a man were to attack me with a knife I would resist him with all my strength, and count it a tragedy if he succeeded. Yet if a surgeon comes to me with a knife, I welcome both him and the knife; let him cut me open, even wider than the knife-attacker, because I know his purpose is good and necessary.

iii. We see further **that the Lord is very compassionate and merciful**. This is not immediately apparent in the story of Job; we can quickly think that God was *cruel* to Job. Yet upon consideration, we can see that God was indeed **very compassionate and merciful**.

- God was **very compassionate and merciful** to Job because He only allowed suffering for a *very good reason*.

- God was **very compassionate and merciful** to Job because He *restricted* what Satan could do against Job.

- God was **very compassionate and merciful** to Job because He *sustained* Him with His unseen hand through all his suffering.

- God was **very compassionate and merciful** to Job because in the whole process God *used* Satan himself. At the end of it all, God had accomplished something wonderful: To make Job a *better* and more *blessed* man than ever. Remember that as good as Job was at the beginning of the book, he was a *better man* at the end of it. He was better in character, humbler, and more blessed than before.

iv. "And when we come to look all Job's life through, we see that *the Lord in mercy brought him out of it all with unspeakable advantage.* He who tested with one hand supported with the other. Whatever Satan's end might be in tempting the patriarch, God had an end which covered and compassed that of the destroyer, and that end was answered all along the line, from the first loss which happened among the oxen to the last taunt of his three accusers." (Spurgeon)

v. **That the Lord is very compassionate**: "I wish we could all read the original Greek; for this word, 'The Lord is very pitiful,' is a specially remarkable one. It means literally that the Lord hath 'many bowels,' or a great heart, and so it indicates great tenderness." (Spurgeon)

4. (12) An exhortation in light of the coming judgment before Jesus.

But above all, my brethren, do not swear, either by heaven or by earth or with any other oath. But let your "Yes," be "Yes," and *your* "No," "No," lest you fall into judgment.

a. **Do not swear**: Many Jewish people in the time James wrote made distinctions between "binding oaths" and "non-binding oaths." Oaths that did not include the name of God were considered non-binding, and to use such oaths was a way of "crossing your fingers behind your back" when telling a lie. It is these kinds of oaths that James condemned.

i. The Bible does not forbid the swearing of all oaths, only against the swearing of deceptive, unwise, or flippant oaths. On occasion God Himself swears oaths (such as in Luke 1:73, Hebrews 3:11, and Hebrews 6:13).

ii. "All swearing is not forbidden, any more than Matthew 5:34; (for oaths are made use of by holy men in both the Old and New Testament, Genesis 21:23, 24; 24:3; 26:28; 1 Kings 17:1-2; 2 Corinthians 1:23; Galatians 1:20; and the use of an oath is permitted and approved of by God himself, Psalm 15:4; Hebrews 6:16) but such oaths are false, rash, vain, without just cause, or customary and frequent in ordinary discourse." (Poole)

b. **Do not swear, either by heaven or by earth or with any other oath**: James again echoed the teaching of Jesus in the Sermon on the Mount (Matthew 5:34-37). The need to swear or make oaths, beyond a simple and clear **yes** or **no** betrays the weakness of one's word. It demonstrates that there is not enough weight in one's own character to confirm their words.

c. **Lest you fall into judgment**: This lack of character will be exposed at the judgment seat of Christ. This motivates us all the more to prepare for that judgment by our speaking with integrity.

i. This admonition may seem out of context to us. Yet, "Probably James jotted it down as an after-thought, to emphasize the warning of James 5:9; in excitement or irritation there was a temptation to curse and swear violently and profanely." (Moffatt)

C. Exhortations for Christians to care for one another.

1. (13-14) How to meet needs arising among Christians.

Is anyone among you suffering? Let him pray. Is anyone cheerful? Let him sing psalms. Is anyone among you sick? Let him call for the elders of the church, and let them pray over him, anointing him with oil in the name of the Lord.

a. **Is anyone among you suffering?** The **suffering** need to pray, the **cheerful** should **sing psalms** of praise to God, and the **sick** should call for the elders of the church, asking them to pray for their need.

i. Instead of *complaining* (as in the previous verse), the sufferer should **pray**. "Instead of murmuring **against one another** (James 5:9), or complaining peevishly, or breaking out into curses, pray to God." (Moffatt)

ii. James has the same advice for both the **suffering** one and the **cheerful** one: take it all to the Lord. In fact, the two commands could be reversed: sufferers should **sing** also, and the cheerful should also **pray**.

iii. "Elsewhere in the N.T. the word **to sing praise** refers to public worship, and always, if the usage in classical Greek and Greek O.T. be decisive, to songs with a musical accompaniment." (Moffatt)

iv. James clearly set the initiative on the person in need: **let *him* call**. The hesitancy of people to ask for or to seek prayer from the leadership of the church in such circumstances is a true mystery.

b. **Let them pray over him**: James also said that the **elders of the church**, as they pray, should anoint the sick person **with oil in the name of the Lord**. This **anointing with oil** has been interpreted as either seeking the best medical attention possible for the afflicted (oil massages were considered medicinal), or as an emblem of the Holy Spirit's presence and power.

i. **Anointing** the sick **with oil** is also mentioned in Mark 6:13. Luke 10:34 mentions the application of oil in a medicinal sense. "The efficacy of olive oil as a medical agent was well known." (Hiebert) According to Burdick, the word for **anoint** here is not the usual one used in the New Testament, but has more of a medicinal meaning to it.

ii. "*Oil* was and is frequently used in the east as a means of cure in very dangerous diseases; and in Egypt it is often used in the cure of the *plague*. Even in Europe it has been tried with great success in the cure of *dropsy*. And *pure olive oil* is excellent for recent wounds and bruises; and I have seen it tried in this way with the best effects. . . . St. James desires them to use *natural means* while looking to God for an especial blessing. And no wise man would direct otherwise." (Clarke)

iii. The Roman Catholic Church mutated this command to anoint the sick into the "sacrament" of Extreme Unction, administered to someone to prepare that one for death. Something James intended to heal was made into a preparation for death!

2. (15-16) God's answer to the prayers of His people.

And the prayer of faith will save the sick, and the Lord will raise him up. And if he has committed sins, he will be forgiven. Confess *your* trespasses to one another, and pray for one another, that you may be healed. The effective, fervent prayer of a righteous man avails much.

a. **And the prayer of faith will save the sick**: Many have wondered if James guarantees healing here for the sick who are prayed for in **faith**. Some interpret this as a reference to ultimate resurrection. The reference to sins being **forgiven** ads to the idea that James is considering a spiritual work and healing, not necessarily a physical healing.

i. Yet the context of the statement demands that James does not *exclude* physical healing as an answer to prayer, though he does seem to mean something broader than *only* a physical healing. We should pray for others in **faith**, expecting that God will heal them, then leave the matter in God's hands.

ii. Clearly, God does not grant immediate healing for every **prayer of faith**, and the reasons are hidden in the heart and mind of God. Still, many are not healed simply because there is no **prayer of faith** offered. The best approach in praying for the sick is to pray with humble confidence that they will be healed, unless God clearly and powerfully makes it clear that this is not His will. Having prayed, we simply leave the matter to God.

iii. Often we do not pray the **prayer of faith** out of concern for God's reputation if there should be no healing. We should remember that God is big enough to handle His own reputation.

b. **Confess your trespasses to one another, and pray for one another, that you may be healed**: James reminds us that mutual confession and prayer brings healing, both physically and spiritually. Confession can free us from the heavy burdens (physically and spiritually) of unresolved sin, and removes hindrances to the work of the Holy Spirit.

i. **To one another**: Confession to another in the body of Christ is essential because sin will demand to have us to itself, isolated from all others. Confession breaks the power of secret sin. Yet, confession need not be made to a "priest" or any imagined mediator; we simply confess **to one another** as appropriate. Confession is good, but must be made with discretion. An unwise confession of sin can be the cause of more sin.

ii. Clarke observes that if this passage actually refers to the Roman Catholic practice of the confessional, then the priest should likewise confess his sins to the people. He also adds: "There is no instance in *auricular confession* where the *penitent* and the *priest* pray together for pardon; but here the people are commanded to pray for each other that they may be healed." (Clarke)

iii. Noting from the context, sin should especially be confessed where physical healing is necessary. It is possible - though by no means always the case - that a person's sickness is the direct result of some sin that has not been dealt with, as Paul describes in 1 Corinthians 11:30.

iv. Hiebert on **confess**: "The root form means literally *to say the same thing*; hence, it means that in confession sin we agree to identify it by its true name and admit that it is sin."

v. "Now, in the primitive church this was openly done as a rule, before the congregation. The earliest manual of the church practice prescribes: 'you must confess your sins in church, and not betake yourself to prayer with a bad conscience' (*Didache* iv.)." (Moffatt)

vi. The great conviction of sin and subsequent confession of sin is common during times of spiritual awakening. There is really nothing unusual about confession during Revival. Finney - a great apostle of Revival - urged it and described it. In the North China revivals under Jonathan Goforth, confession was almost invariably the prelude to blessing; one writer describing the significant Korean revivals associated with Goforth wrote: *"We may have our theories of the desirability or undesirability of public confession of sin. I have had mine, but I know that when the Spirit of God falls upon guilty souls, there will be confession, and no power on earth can stop it."* (from *Calling to Remembrance* by William Newton Blair)

vii. Public confession of sin has the potential for great good or bad. Some guiding principles can help.

- *Confession should be made to the one sinned against.* "Most Christians display a preference for confession in secret before God, even concerning matters which involve other people. To confess to God seems to them to be the easiest way out. If offenders were really conscious of the presence of God, even secret confession of private sin would have a good effect. Alas, most offenders merely commune with themselves instead of making contact with God, who refuses their prayers under certain conditions. In the words of our Lord, it is clear that sin involving another person should be confessed to that person." (Orr)

- *Confession should often be public.* James 5:16 illustrates this principle. A.T. Robertson, the great Greek scholar, says that in James 5:16 the odd tense of the Greek verb **confess** in this verse implies group confession rather than private confession. It is confession "ones to others" not "one to one other."

- *Public confession must be discrete.* Often the confession needs to be no more than what is necessary to enlist prayer. It can be enough to say publicly, "Pray for me, I need victory over my besetting sin." It would be wrong to go into more detail, but saying this much is important. It keeps us from being "let's pretend Christians" who act as if everything is fine when it isn't. "Almost all sexual transgressions are either secret or private and should be so confessed. A burden too great to bear may be shared with a pastor or doctor or a friend of the same sex. Scripture discourages even the naming of immorality among believers, and declares that it is a shame even to speak of things done in secret by the immoral." (Orr)

- *Distinguish between secret sins and those which directly affect others.* Orr gives a good principle: "If you sin secretly, confess secretly, admitting publicly that you need the victory but keeping details to yourself. If you sin openly confess openly to remove stumbling blocks from those whom you have hindered. If you have sinned spiritually (prayerlessness, lovelessness, and unbelief as well as their offspring, criticism, etc.) then confess to the church that you have been a hindrance." (J. Edwin Orr)

- *Confession is often made to people, but before God.* At the same time, we notice that James says **confess your trespasses to one another**. One of the interesting things about confession of sin as I have noticed it in the writings of J. Edwin Orr is that the confessions are almost always addressed to *people*, not to *God*. It isn't that you confess your sin to God and others merely hear. You confess your sin before others and ask them to pray for you to get it right before God.

- *Confession should be appropriately specific.* When open confession of sin is appropriate - more than the public stating of spiritual need, but confessing open sin or sin against the church - it must be *specific.* "*If* I made any mistakes I'm sorry" is no confession of sin at all. You sinned specifically, so confess specifically. "It costs nothing for a church member to admit in a prayer meeting: 'I am not what I ought to be.' It costs no more to say: 'I ought to be a better Christian.' It costs something to say: 'I have been a trouble-maker in this church.' It costs something to say: 'I have had bitterness of heart towards certain leaders, to whom I shall definitely apologise.' " (Orr, *Full Surrender*)

- *Confession should be thorough.* "Some confessions are not thorough. They are too general. They are not made to the persons concerned. They neglect completely the necessary restitution. Or they make no provision for a different course of conduct in which the sin is forsaken. They are endeavours for psychological relief." (Orr)

- *Confession must have honesty and integrity.* If we confess with no real intention of battling the sin, our confession isn't thorough and it mocks God. The story is told of an Irishman who confessed to his priest that he had stolen two bags of potatoes. The priest had heard the gossip around town and said to the man, "Mike, I heard it was only one bag of potatoes stolen from the market." The Irishman replied, "That's true Father, but it was so easy that I plan on taking another tomorrow night." *By all means, avoid phony confession - confession without true brokenness or sorrow. If it isn't deeply real, it isn't any good.*

- *One need not fear that public confession of sin will inevitably get out of hand.* Orr tells of a time when a woman was overwrought by deep sorrow for sin and became hysterical. He saw the danger immediately and told her, "Quiet, sister. Turn your eyes on Jesus." She did and the danger of extreme emotion was avoided.

- *Those who hear a confession of sin also have a great responsibility.* Those who hear the confession should have the proper response: loving, intercessory prayer, and not human wisdom, gossiping, or "sharing" the need with others.

viii. According to Moffatt, the English Prayer Book, before the communion service, the minister is to give this invitation: "Come to me or to some other discreet and learned minister of God's Word, and open his grief; that by the ministry of God's holy Word he may receive the benefit of absolution." There can be great value to *opening one's grief.*

ix. Real, deep, genuine confession of sin has been a feature of every genuine awakening or revival in the past 250 years. But it isn't anything new, as demonstrated by the revival in Ephesus recorded in Acts 19:17-20. It says, *many who believed came confessing and telling their deeds.* This was *Christians* getting right with God, and open confession was part of it.

c. **The effective, fervent prayer of a righteous man avails much**: In writing about the need for prayer for the suffering, for the sick, and for the sinning, James points to the **effective** nature of prayer - when it is **fervent** and offered by a **righteous man**.

i. The idea of **fervent** in this context is *strong.* "It might be rendered literally: 'Very strong is the supplication of a righteous man, energizing.'" (Meyer)

ii. "When such a power of prayer is granted, faith should be immediately called into exercise, that the blessing may be given: the spirit of prayer is the proof that the power of God is present to heal. *Long prayers* give no particular evidence of *Divine inspiration.*" (Clarke)

iii. Much of our prayer is not effective simply because it is not **fervent**. It is offered with a lukewarm attitude that virtually asks God to care about something that we care little about. Effective prayer must be **fervent**, not because we must emotionally persuade a reluctant God, but because we must gain God's heart by being **fervent** for the things He is **fervent** for.

iv. Additionally, effective prayer is offered by a **righteous man**. This is someone who recognizes the grounds of his righteousness reside in Jesus, and whose personal walk is generally consistent with the righteousness that he has in Jesus.

v. **Avails much**: "It was so with John Knox, whose prayers were more dreaded by Mary of Scots than the armies of Philip." (Meyer)

3. (17-18) Elijah as an example of answered prayer.

Elijah was a man with a nature like ours, and he prayed earnestly that it would not rain; and it did not rain on the land for three years and six months. And he prayed again, and the heaven gave rain, and the earth produced its fruit.

a. **Elijah was a man with a nature like ours**: Elijah is a model of earnest prayer that was answered by God. His effectiveness in prayer extended even to the weather! Yet this shows that Elijah's heart was in tune with God's. He prayed for the rain to stop and start only because he sensed it was in the heart of God in His dealings with Israel.

b. **Prayed earnestly**: Literally, this is *prayed with prayer*. To truly pray, by definition, is to pray **earnestly**.

i. *"He prayed with prayer*, a Hebraism for, he *prayed fervently."* (Clarke)

c. **Elijah was a man with a nature like ours**: This being true, we then can be men with the power of prayer like him.

4. (19-20) Helping a sinning brother.

Brethren, if anyone among you wanders from the truth, and someone turns him back, let him know that he who turns a sinner from the error of his way will save a soul from death and cover a multitude of sins.

a. **If anyone among you wanders from the truth**: Having introduced the topics of sin and confession, James reminds us of the need to confront those who have wandered from the truth. **Wanders from the truth** is a good picture. Most people don't wander deliberately - it just sort of happens. Nonetheless, it still gets them off track and possibly in danger.

i. "Read the verse and you will see that it was that of a backslider from the visible church of God. The words, 'If any of you,' must refer to a professed Christian." (Spurgeon)

b. **And someone turns him back**: This shows us that God uses human instruments in turning sinners back from the errors of their ways. God does not need to use such human instruments, and sometimes He does not. The Apostle Paul – or rather, Saul of Tarsus – was not converted through any human instrument, save perhaps the prayers of the dying martyr Stephen for him. Yet no one preached to him, but Jesus decided to meet him directly.

i. One reason God uses human instruments is because it brings Him *more* glory than if He were to do His work by Himself. In this way God is like a skilled workman who makes incredible things using the *worst* of tools. After the same pattern, God uses earthen vessels to be containers of His glory.

ii. "Most persons have been convinced by the pious conversation of sisters, by the holy example of mothers, by the minister, by the Sabbath-school, or by the reading of tracts or perusing Scripture. Let us not therefore believe that God will often work without instruments;

let us not sit down silently and say, 'God will do his own work.' It is quite true he will; but then he does his work by using his children as instruments." (Spurgeon)

iii. Along this line, can we not say that when we refuse to make ourselves available to God's service – weak and failing as we are – we in fact *rob* Him of some of His glory? He can glorify Himself through a weak vessel like you; you should let Him do it.

iv. "It may not appear so brilliant a thing to bring back a backslider as to reclaim a harlot or a drunkard, but in the sight of God it is no small miracle of grace, and to the instrument who has performed it shall yield no small comfort. Seek ye, then, my brethren, those who were of us but have gone from us; seek ye those who linger still in the congregation but have disgraced the church, and are put away from us, and rightly so, because we cannot countenance their uncleanness; seek them with prayers, and tears, and entreaties, if peradventure God may grant them repentance that they may be saved." (Spurgeon)

c. **He who turns a sinner from the error of his way will save a soul from death and cover a multitude of sins**: There is a blessing for the one who loves his brother enough to confront him, and who turns him from **the error of his way**. He has saved that **soul from death** and covered **a multitude of sins**.

i. This speaks powerfully of the *restoration* that is possible for those who have sinned. "I know of men of good standing in the gospel ministry, who, ten years ago, fell into sin; and that is thrown in our teeth to this very day. Do you speak of them? You are at once informed, 'Why, ten years ago they did so-and-so.' Brethren, Christian men ought to be ashamed of themselves for taking notice of such things so long afterwards. True, we may use more caution in our dealings; but to reproach a fallen brother for what he did so long ago, is contrary to the spirit of John, who went after Peter, three days after he had denied his Master with oaths and curses." (Spurgeon)

ii. James concludes with this because this is exactly what he has endeavored to do through this challenging letter - to confront those who have wandered from a living faith, endeavoring to save their souls from death, by demanding that they not only hear the word, but do it, because a living faith will have its proof.

iii. "So the homily ends – abruptly, even more abruptly than the First Epistle of John, without any closing word of farewell to the readers, abruptly but not ineffectively. The Wisdom writings on which it is modeled end as suddenly." (Moffatt)

1 Peter 1 - Living like You are Born Again

A. A greeting from the Apostle Peter.

1. (1) The writer and the intended readers of this letter.

Peter, an apostle of Jesus Christ, to the pilgrims of the Dispersion in Pontus, Galatia, Cappadocia, Asia, and Bithynia,

a. **Peter**: He was not merely **an apostle**, but there is a sense in which he was the *leader* of the apostolic group. Peter was an important and influential man in the early church. Considering the author, the first Christians would receive this letter with a sense of importance.

i. Peter's name is mentioned in the gospels more than anyone except the name of Jesus. No one speaks in the gospels as often as Peter did, and Jesus spoke more to Peter than to any other individual.

- Jesus rebuked Peter more than any other disciple.

- Peter was the only disciple who dared to rebuke Jesus.

- Peter confessed Jesus more boldly and accurately than any other disciple.

- Peter denied Jesus more forcefully and publicly than any other disciple.

- Jesus praised Peter more than any other disciple.

- Jesus addressed Peter as Satan alone among the disciples.

ii. Since Peter is so prominent in the gospel records, it is worthwhile to remind ourselves of some of the important mentions of Peter in the record of Biblical history.

- When Jesus woke up early in the morning to pray before the sun came up, Simon Peter led the other disciples on a hunt to find Jesus and tell Him what He should do (Mark 1:35-39).

- Peter put his nets out at the direction of Jesus to bring in a massive catch of fish (Luke 5:1-11).

- Peter went on a unique outreach trip with the other disciples (Matthew 10:1-42).

- Peter stepped out of the boat during a raging storm and walked on the water with Jesus (Matthew 14:24-33).

- Peter was the one who said, *"Lord, to whom shall we go? You have the words of eternal life. Also, we have come to believe and to know that You are the Christ, the Son of the living God"* (John 6:68-69).

- Peter saw Jesus transfigured in glory, together with Moses and Elijah (Matthew 17:1-9).

- Peter was the one who asked Jesus how many times we should forgive a brother that sins against us, quoting the high number of "seven times" (Matthew 18:21-35).

- Peter was the one who asked Jesus, after the encounter with the rich young ruler, what the disciples would receive for giving everything up to follow Jesus (Matthew 19:27-30).

- Peter was the one who insisted that Jesus would not wash his feet; then he commanded Jesus to wash his whole body! (John 13:16-20).

- Peter heard Jesus predict that he would deny Him three times (Matthew 26:30-35), and Peter replied, *"Even if I have to die with you I will not deny You!"* (Matthew 26:35), and the rest of the disciples agreed.

- Peter was the one who cut off the *right* ear of Malchus, the servant of the high priest, when the soldiers came to arrest Jesus (John 18:1-11).

- Peter denied Jesus three times, cursing and swearing that he did not even know "the Man," refusing to even name the name of Jesus (Matthew 26:69-75).

- Peter was the one who ran with John the disciple to the tomb on the morning of the resurrection, after hearing the report of the women that the body of Jesus was not in its tomb (John 20:1-10).

- Peter was the one who received a personal visit from the resurrected Jesus on the day of the resurrection (Luke 24:34).

- Peter received a public restoration of Jesus in front of the other disciples after the resurrection of Jesus (John 21).

iii. Significantly, Peter introduced himself as an **apostle**. "The supreme importance of the apostles is suggested by the fact that the phrase *of Jesus Christ* is attached to no other New Testament office: we do not read of *teachers of Jesus Christ* or *prophets of Jesus Christ* or *evangelists of Jesus Christ*, only of *apostles of Jesus Christ*." (Grudem)

iv. Peter did nothing to explain or justify his apostleship and did not add a phrase like "by the will of God" as Paul did on some occasions (1 Corinthians 1:1, 2 Corinthians 1:1, Galatians 1:1, Ephesians 1:1, and so on). "Unlike Paul, Peter's apostolic status was never questioned. This brief phrase indicates Peter's authority." (Hiebert)

b. **To the pilgrims**: The idea behind the word **pilgrims** is of someone who lives as *a temporary resident in a foreign land*. **Pilgrims** are sojourners and travelers, and **pilgrims** live in constant awareness of their true home.

i. The early Christian writing *The Epistle to Diognetus* gives the idea of what **pilgrims** are. "They inhabit the lands of their birth, but as temporary residents of it; they take their share of all responsibilities as citizens, and endure all disabilities as aliens. Every foreign land is their native land, and every native land a foreign land . . . they pass their days upon earth, but their citizenship is in heaven." (Cited in Barclay)

c. **To the pilgrims of the Dispersion**: Peter clearly wrote to Gentiles, Christians (see 1 Peter 1:18, 2:10, and 4:3). Yet he called them **pilgrims of the Dispersion**, a name that was applied to the Jews. He called them this because he saw the Christians of his day as sprinkled throughout the world as the Jewish people were in **the Dispersion** after the fall of Jerusalem when the Babylonians conquered Judah.

d. **Pontus, Galatia, Cappadocia, Asia, and Bithynia**: These specific areas were places Christianity had extended in the first several decades after the beginning of the church. It was probably the route that the original courier of Peter's letter followed in distributing the letter. This was not written to any one congregation, but intentionally written to *all* Christians.

2. (2) Peter's description of his readers and all Christians.

Elect according to the foreknowledge of God the Father, in sanctification of the Spirit, for obedience and sprinkling of the blood of Jesus Christ: Grace to you and peace be multiplied.

a. **Elect according to the foreknowledge**: Peter first described his intended readers as **elect**. This means simply that they are *chosen*, chosen by God in a particular and unique sense.

i. "The opening characterization of the readers as elect was meant to strengthen and encourage them in their affliction. The doctrine of

election is a 'family truth' intended to foster the welfare of believers."
(Hiebert)

b. **According to the foreknowledge of God**: This describes the nature of
their election. God's choosing is not random or uninformed, but **according** to His **foreknowledge**, which is an aspect of His omniscience. This
foreknowledge *includes* prior knowledge of our response to the gospel, but
is not *solely dependent* on it.

i. Though God's election is **according to . . . foreknowledge**, there is
more to His foreknowledge than His prior knowledge of my response
to Jesus. Election is not election at all if it is only a cause-and-effect
arrangement basing God's choice only on man's.

c. **In sanctification of the Spirit, for obedience**: An essential result of
election is **sanctification** and **obedience**. While some would like to think
that election has only to do with going to heaven or hell, Peter reminds
us that it also touches earth. A claim to be among the **elect** is doubtful if
there is no evidence of **sanctification** and **obedience**.

d. **And sprinkling of the blood of Jesus Christ**: However, since all the elect
fall short of perfect sanctification and obedience, there is cleansing from sin
provided for them through the **sprinkling of the blood of Jesus Christ**.

i. There were three circumstances in the Old Testament where blood
was sprinkled on people.

• At the establishment of Sinai or Old Covenant (Exodus
24:5-8).

• At the ordination of Aaron and his sons (Exodus 29:21).

• At the purification ceremony for a cleansed leper (Leviticus
14:6-7).

ii. The **sprinkling of the blood of Jesus** on us accomplishes the same
things. First, a covenant is formed, then we are ordained as priests to
Him, and finally we are cleansed from our corruption and sin. Each
of these is ours through the work of Jesus on the cross.

e. **God the Father . . . the Spirit . . . Jesus Christ**: Peter's effortless way of
combining the work of the Father, Son, and Holy Spirit in our salvation
displays the New Testament approach to the Trinity. It is not detailed as a
specific doctrine, but woven into the fabric of the New Testament.

i. Jesus has a **Father**, but not in the sense of being higher than He or
the One who gave Him existence. The Father, the Son, and the Holy
Spirit have existed together throughout eternity and each is equally
God. **Father** and *Son* are terms used to describe the *relationship* between
these first two members of the Trinity.

f. **Grace to you and peace be multiplied**: Peter brought a greeting that had become common among the Christians, combining elements from Greek culture (**Grace**) and Jewish culture (**peace**).

B. What it means to be saved and to live saved.

1. (3-5) Thanks to the Father for His work of salvation.

Blessed *be* the God and Father of our Lord Jesus Christ, who according to His abundant mercy has begotten us again to a living hope through the resurrection of Jesus Christ from the dead, to an inheritance incorruptible and undefiled and that does not fade away, reserved in heaven for you, who are kept by the power of God through faith for salvation ready to be revealed in the last time.

a. **Blessed be the God and Father of our Lord Jesus Christ**: When Peter considered the salvation of God, his immediate response was to simply praise Him. This is especially because the motive for God's work is found in Him, not in us (being **according to His abundant mercy**).

i. Hiebert says of the extended passage 1 Peter 1:3-12: "This beautiful passage is the outpouring of an adorning heart. Only one who has devoutly contemplated the greatness of our salvation could utter such a magnificent paean of praise, one that prepares and encourages the suffering soul to steadfastly continue the spiritual battle."

ii. All His goodness to us begins with **mercy**. "No other attribute could have helped us had mercy been refused. As we are by nature, justice condemns us, holiness frowns upon us, power crushes us, truth confirms the threatening of the law, and wrath fulfils it. It is from the mercy of our God that all our hopes begin." (Spurgeon)

b. **Has begotten us again**: The wording of **begotten us again** is different from *born again* (John 3:3) but the meaning is the same. Peter's idea is that when a person is saved, they are made a *new creation* (as in 2 Corinthians 5:17).

c. **To a living hope**: We are born again to **a living hope** because we have eternal life in a Savior who has conquered death Himself. The hope lives because it is set upon an **inheritance incorruptible** that can never **fade away** because it is **reserved in heaven**. This is a significant contrast to any inheritance on this earth.

i. "It is also called a 'living hope,' because it is imperishable. Other hopes fade like withering flowers. The hopes of the rich, the boasts of the proud, all these will die out as a candle when it flickers in the socket. The hope of the greatest monarch has been crushed before our eyes; he set up the standard of victory too soon, and has seen it trailed in the mire. There is no unwaning hope beneath the changeful moon:

the only imperishable hope is that which climbs above the stars, and fixes itself upon the throne of God and the person of Jesus Christ." (Spurgeon)

d. **Incorruptible and undefiled and that does not fade away**: Peter didn't really describe our inheritance. All he can tell us is what it is *not*. What our inheritance actually *is* is something too great for him to describe. Yet we can know that our inheritance can't *perish*, it can't *spoil*, and it can't **fade away**.

i. Our inheritance is like the inheritance of Aaron (Numbers 18:20) and the inheritance of the Psalmist (Psalm 16:5-6), which is the gift of God Himself. Since God gives Himself to us now, our inheritance begins here and now.

ii. We cannot experience this inheritance unless we are born again. Unregenerate man does not have the *capacity* to enjoy this inheritance. It would be like rewarding a blind man by showing him the most beautiful sunset or taking him to an art museum.

iii. In speaking with those who don't know Jesus we shouldn't just tell them of the agonies of hell they will experience, but also of the glories of heaven they will miss.

e. **Who are kept by the power of God through faith**: The promise of our inheritance is certain because we **are kept by the power of God**. This enables us to endure **through faith** until the coming of Jesus.

i. "God's power is the garrison in which we find our security." (Hiebert) We are **kept by the power of God**, but it is **through faith**, meaning our faith. The person who is **kept** is a person abiding in a continuing relationship of **faith** with God. We could say that **faith** activates the preserving power of God in the life of the Christian.

ii. "To have been told, as in the preceding verse, that our inheritance was *reserved in heaven* could have yielded us little comfort, unless that assurance had been followed and capped by this, that the heirs also are being kept for its full enjoyment." (Meyer)

2. (6-9) The purpose of trials for those who are saved.

In this you greatly rejoice, though now for a little while, if need be, you have been grieved by various trials, that the genuineness of your faith, *being* much more precious than gold that perishes, though it is tested by fire, may be found to praise, honor, and glory at the revelation of Jesus Christ, whom having not seen you love. Though now you do not see *Him*, yet believing, you rejoice with joy inexpressible and full of glory, receiving the end of your faith; the salvation of *your* souls.

a. **In this you greatly rejoice**: We especially **rejoice** in God's keeping power when we are **grieved by various trials**, knowing that He will keep us as our faith is **tested by fire**.

> i. **If need be, you have been grieved**: Sometimes it is thought that a strong Christian will never be **grieved** in a trial. The idea is that a Christian should be like Superman; though bullets are shot at Superman, they all bounce off of his chest. Yet Peter here tells us that there is a "**need be**" not only for the **various trials**, but more especially that there is a "**need be**" for being **grieved** itself. God has a purpose not only for the trial but also for the heavy grief we feel in the trial.

> ii. **Various trials**: "Literally, it means 'many-colored' and was used to describe 'the skin of a leopard, the different-colored veinings of marble, or an embroidered robe.'" (Hiebert)

b. **Faith . . . tested by fire**: Our **faith** isn't tested because God doesn't know how much or what kind of faith we have. It is **tested** because *we* often are ignorant of how much or what kind of faith we have. God's purpose in testing is to display the enduring quality of our faith.

> i. "Indeed, it is the honor of faith to be tried. Shall any man say, 'I have faith, but I have never had to believe under difficulties'? Who knows whether thou hast any faith? Shall a man say, 'I have great faith in God, but I have never had to use it in anything more than the ordinary affairs of life, where I could probably have done without it as well as with it'? Is this to the honor and praise of thy faith? Dost thou think that such a faith as this will bring any great glory to God, or bring to thee any great reward? If so, thou art mightily mistaken." (Spurgeon)

> ii. **Much more precious than gold that perishes**: If **gold** is fit to be tested and purified by fire, then how **much more** our faith, which is far **more precious than gold**? God has a great and important purpose in testing our faith.

> - Faith is tested to show that it is sincere faith or true faith.
> - Faith is tested to show the strength of faith.
> - Faith is tested to purify it, to burn away the dross from the gold.

> iii. **Gold** is one of the most durable of all materials. Yet it too will one day perish, but our faith will not.

c. **Receiving the end of your faith**: The **end of your faith** is the return of Jesus and the ultimate **salvation of your souls**. Testing and trials are inevitable as long as we are on this side of **the end of your faith**. As long as we do not see the God we serve we must endure through trials and face them with faith and joy.

i. **Whom having not seen you love**: Peter knew that though he had seen Jesus (both before and after the resurrection) most every Christian in the early church had **not seen** Jesus. Nevertheless, they loved Him. Jesus was no less real because they had not seen Him.

ii. "In short, there is an equality between the believers in the present time, and those who lived in the time of the incarnation; for Christ, to a believing soul, is the same *to-day* that he was *yesterday* and will be *for ever*." (Clarke)

iii. The word translated "**joy inexpressible**" "occurs only here in the New Testament, and describes a joy so profound as to be beyond the power of words to express." (Grudem) "Their joy was no ordinary, earth-born joy." (Hiebert)

3. (10-12) The prior revelation of the salvation experienced by Christians.

Of this salvation the prophets have inquired and searched carefully, who prophesied of the grace *that would come* to you, searching what, or what manner of time, the Spirit of Christ who was in them was indicating when He testified beforehand the sufferings of Christ and the glories that would follow. To them it was revealed that, not to themselves, but to us they were ministering the things which now have been reported to you through those who have preached the gospel to you by the Holy Spirit sent from heaven; things which angels desire to look into.

a. **Of this salvation the prophets have inquired and searched carefully**: It was important to Peter – and to all the New Testament writers – to demonstrate that their teaching was no novelty, but that it was **testified beforehand** by the prophets. Understanding this made salvation so much greater in the mind of Peter's afflicted readers.

i. "Peter did not seek to prove the truth of his teaching about salvation by showing its agreements with the prophets; rather, he sought to encourage his afflicted readers by demonstrating the importance and comprehensive grandeur of the salvation for which they were being afflicted." (Hiebert)

b. **Prophesied of the grace that would come to you**: The prophets of the Old Testament longed to see the **grace** of the New Covenant to come. Prophesying by the **Spirit of Christ**, they knew *something* of His **sufferings** and **glories**, but far less than they longed to know.

i. One may only imagine how excited Isaiah would have been to read the Gospel of John. The Old Testament prophets knew so much; yet much was hidden to them, including the character of the Church (Ephesians 3:4-6) and the very essence of life and immortality (2 Timothy 1:10).

c. **To them it was revealed that, not to themselves, but to us they were ministering**: The prophets understood that **they were ministering** to people beyond them as well as to people in their own day. These things the prophets predicted were reported as fact by the apostles (**the things which now have been reported to you through those who have preached the gospel**).

> i. Because we know the *Who* (Jesus) and the *when* (Jesus' day) of these Old Testament prophecies, they should be of far more interest to us than they were even in the day of the prophets.

d. **Things which angels desire to look into**: The unfolding of God's eternal plan is something that **angels desire to look into**. Angels observe our conduct (1 Corinthians 4:9), making it necessary that Christians conduct themselves properly (1 Corinthians 11:10).

> i. Part of God's eternal purpose is to show His wisdom to the angelic beings through His work with the church (Ephesians 3:10-11). God *wants* the angels to **look** in on what He does in the church, and the idea is that the angels are bending over with intense interest and **desire** to learn.

> ii. Therefore, they **desire** to see and learn. This word "Denotes a strong interest or craving. The present tense portrays a present, continued inner yearning to comprehend. The term does not imply that the desire cannot or should not be fulfilled, but it does mark an enduring angelic effort to comprehend more of the mystery of human salvation." (Hiebert)

> iii. "The longing must therefore include a holy curiosity to watch and delight in the glories of Christ's kingdom as they find ever fuller realization in their lives of individual Christians throughout the history of the church." (Grudem)

> iv. "First Corinthians 4:9, Ephesians 3:10, and 1 Timothy 3:16 likewise picture the supernatural world eagerly observing God's program of human redemption. The concept seems grounded in Jesus' words in Luke 15:7, 10 where angels are said to rejoice over one repentant sinner." (Hiebert)

4. (13-17) The conduct of those who are saved.

Therefore gird up the loins of your mind, be sober, and rest *your* hope fully upon the grace that is to be brought to you at the revelation of Jesus Christ; as obedient children, not conforming yourselves to the former lusts, *as* in your ignorance; but as He who called you *is* holy, you also be holy in all *your* conduct, because it is written, "Be holy, for I am holy." And if you call on the Father, who without partiality judges

according to each one's work, conduct yourselves throughout the time of your stay *here* in fear;

a. **Therefore gird up the loins of your mind**: Living the way God wants us to means that we must **gird up the loins** of our **mind**. The idea in this phrase is to prepare for action, much like the phrase "rolling up your sleeves." Then we must also be **sober**, which means the ability to take a serious look at life.

i. To **gird up the loins of your mind** is to get rid of loose and sloppy thinking; to bring the rational and reflective powers of your mind under control. It means to control what you think about, those things you decide to set your mind upon.

ii. **Be sober**: "It denotes a condition free from every form of mental and spiritual loss of self-control; it is an attitude of self-discipline that avoids the extremes." (Hiebert)

b. **Rest your hope fully upon the grace that is to be brought to you at the revelation of Jesus Christ**: Peter has told us a lot about God's grace. He greeted us with grace (1 Peter 1:2). He told us of the grace that came to us in Jesus, predicted by the prophets of old (1 Peter 1:10). Now he goes further, writing of **the grace that is to be brought to you** when Jesus comes back. The only way we will be able to stand before Jesus on that day is because of the *unmerited favor* He gives and will give to us.

i. **Grace** isn't just for the past, when we first gave our lives to Jesus. It isn't only for the present, where we live each moment standing in His grace (Romans 5:2). It is also for the future, when **grace** will be **brought to us**. God has only just *begun* to show us the riches of His grace.

ii. "*Grace* is the unmerited love of God, stooping to save and bless; the source of all those bright and holy gifts which come from his infinite heart." (Meyer)

c. **As obedient children, not conforming yourselves to the former lusts, as in your ignorance**: Fulfilling God's call to holiness requires that we, **as obedient children**, break off with the lifestyle of the world (which is characterized by **lusts** and **ignorance**).

d. **But as He who called you is holy, you also be holy in all your conduct, because it is written, "Be holy, for I am holy"**: The main idea behind *holiness* is not moral purity but it is the idea of "*apartness*." The idea is that God is *separate*, different from His creation, both in His essential nature and in the perfection of His attributes. But instead of building a wall around His apartness, God calls us to come to Him and share His apartness. He says to us, **"Be holy, for I am holy."**

i. When we fail to see God's apartness, we begin to believe that He is just a "super-man." Then we don't see that His love is a **holy** love, His justice is a **holy** justice, and so on with all of His attributes. Holiness is not so much something we possess as it is something that possesses us.

ii. In this, the God of the Bible is radically different from the pagan gods commonly worshipped in New Testament times. "Heathenism scarcely produced a god whose example was not the most abominable; their greatest gods, especially, were paragons of impurity." (Clarke)

e. **And if you call on the Father**: If we as Christians **call on** a holy God (presumably for help), we must understand that we call on a God who shows no **partiality** - and will so judge our conduct. This makes a working, sober, holy walk all the more important.

5. (18-21) The motivation for godly living.

Knowing that you were not redeemed with corruptible things, *like* **silver or gold, from your aimless conduct** *received* **by tradition from your fathers, but with the precious blood of Christ, as of a lamb without blemish and without spot. He indeed was foreordained before the foundation of the world, but was manifest in these last times for you who through Him believe in God, who raised Him from the dead and gave Him glory, so that your faith and hope are in God.**

a. **Knowing that you were not redeemed with corruptible things**: The high call for godly living makes sense in light of the price that was paid for our redemption. The precious blood of Jesus did not save us so that we could then live as if we were garbage.

b. **From your aimless conduct received by tradition from your fathers**: Peter described the frame of mind which seeks to be justified by law as **aimless conduct**. It seems to have an *aim* – gaining merit before God by works – but it is in fact **aimless** because it cannot succeed.

c. **A lamb without blemish and without spot**: Peter here spoke in reference to the completely sinless character of Jesus. If He were not **without blemish and without spot**, He would not have been qualified to be our Redeemer.

d. **He indeed was foreordained before the foundation of the world**: The work of Jesus was not a plan developed late in the course of redemption. It **was foreordained before the foundation of the world**, though it was made evident **in these last times**.

e. **For you who through Him believe in God**: The entire plan of redemption is for those who **believe in God**, though even their belief is **through Him**. Those who **believe in God** are not disappointed because their faith and hope has been substantiated by Jesus' resurrection **from the dead**.

6. (22-25) The necessity for love among the saved.

Since you have purified your souls in obeying the truth through the Spirit in sincere love of the brethren, love one another fervently with a pure heart, having been born again, not of corruptible seed but incorruptible, through the word of God which lives and abides forever, because "All flesh *is* as grass, and all the glory of man as the flower of the grass. The grass withers, and its flower falls away, but the word of the LORD endures forever." Now this is the word which by the gospel was preached to you.

a. **Love one another fervently**: Holy living is incomplete if it is not accompanied by **love**. To be a Christian means to have a **sincere love of the brethren**, but we are encouraged to exercise that love **fervently**.

b. **Love one another fervently with a pure heart, having been born again**: Such love is only possible (and only to be expected) of those who have been **born again** by the eternal word of God.

i. Again, Peter did not use the same wording for **born again** as is found in John 3; but he did use the exact same idea.

c. **Through the word of God which lives and abides forever**: We are **born again . . . through the word of God**. But it doesn't only give us new life. It also tells us to **love one another**. If the word of God is as Isaiah 40:8 says it is - **the word of the Lord which endures forever**, then we are both obligated by it and empowered by it, to live out the kind of love and holiness Peter speaks of.

d. **The grass withers, and its flower falls away, but the word of the LORD endures forever**: Peter here quoted from Isaiah 40:6-8. **The word of the LORD** certainly *has* endured. It has survived centuries of manual transcription, of persecution, of ever changing philosophies, of all kinds of critics, of neglect both in the pulpit and in the pew, of doubt and disbelief - and still, **the word of the LORD endures forever!**

i. In AD 303 the Roman Emperor Diocletian demanded that every copy of the Scriptures in the Roman Empire be burned. He failed, and 25 years later the Roman Emperor Constantine commissioned a scholar named Eusebius to prepare 50 copies of the Bible at government expense.

ii. "A thousand times over, the death knell of the Bible has been sounded, the funeral procession formed, the inscription cut on the tombstone, and committal read. But somehow the corpse never stays put." (Bernard Ramm, *Protestant Christian Evidences*)

iii. "God's Word never dies, God's Word never changes. There are some who think we ought to get a new gospel every few years or even every few weeks, but that was not Peter's notion. He wrote, and he was divinely inspired to write, concerning 'the Word of God, which liveth and abideth for ever.'" (Spurgeon)

iv. Since this eternal, always potentially fruit-bearing seed is in us, we have both the *obligation* and the *ability* to have a **sincere love of the brethren**. Perhaps we could say that if we need more love towards others it begins with having more of the **incorruptible seed** set in our hearts and allowed to grow.

e. **Through the word of God . . . Now this is the word**: Some people try to draw a sharp distinction between the two Greek words most often translated **word**, which are the ancient Greek words *rhema* and *logos*. But here Peter used both words (*logos* in 1 Peter 1:23 and *rhema* in 1 Peter 1:25) to refer to the exact same idea. The two words sometimes have subtle differences, but often not significant differences.

1 Peter 2 - The Glory and the Duty of God's People

A. Coming to Jesus through His word.

1. (1-3) How to respond to the eternal word of God.

Therefore, laying aside all malice, all deceit, hypocrisy, envy, and all evil speaking, as newborn babes, desire the pure milk of the word, that you may grow thereby, if indeed you have tasted that the Lord *is* gracious.

a. **Therefore**: Peter has just demonstrated the glory and eternal character of God's word. Now **therefore**, in light of what God's word is to us, we should receive the word and receive it with a particular heart.

b. **As newborn babes, desire the pure milk of the word**: The word **desire** is strong. In the Septuagint (an ancient Greek translation of the Old Testament) it is used for man's deepest longing for God: *As the deer <u>pants</u> for the water brooks, so <u>pants</u> my soul for You, O God* (Psalm 42:1). It speaks of the **desire** each believer should have for the word of God.

i. **Babes . . . desire**: A healthy new baby has an instinctive yearning for its mother's milk. When things are right, you don't have to tell it to want the milk.

ii. The failure to either **desire** or to *receive* this **pure milk of the word** is the reason for so many problems in both individual Christian lives and in congregations. "The sickly condition of so many Christians sets forth a lamentable complaint of the food with which they are supplied. To say nothing of strong meat, they do not even get milk. Hence the Church of God too much resembles the wards of a children's hospital." (Meyer)

c. **That you may grow thereby**: The Word of God is necessary for the growth of the Christian. We should all **desire the pure milk of the word**, even though Paul rebukes the Corinthians for being able to *only* receive milk (1 Corinthians 3:1-2), the Christian should *never* get tired of the simple truths of the Gospel simply presented.

i. Who are the **newborn babes**? In a sense, we all are. "The most advanced among us, in knowledge and attainment, are, in comparison with what they shall be, only as babes." (Meyer)

ii. "To drink the milk of the Word is to 'taste' again and again what he is like, for in the hearing of the Lord's words believers experience the joy of personal fellowship with the Lord himself." (Grudem)

d. **Laying aside all malice, guile, hypocrisy, envy, and all evil speaking**: This described the attitude of heart that receives the word and grows by the word. This is a humble, honest heart, willing to *do* what the Word of God says.

i. **Evil speaking**: This ancient Greek word has more the idea of spicy and hurtful gossip than the idea of profane speech.

e. **If indeed you have tasted that the Lord is gracious**: If we have received from God and have **tasted** (personally experienced) **that the Lord is gracious**, then we have great reason and responsibility to receive the word in the enthusiastic way that babies receive their milk.

2. (4-5) Coming to Jesus.

Coming to Him *as to* a living stone, rejected indeed by men, but chosen by God *and* precious, you also, as living stones, are being built up a spiritual house, a holy priesthood, to offer up spiritual sacrifices acceptable to God through Jesus Christ.

a. **Coming to Him as to a living stone**: Peter's picture here is that God is building a spiritual temple (**a spiritual house**) using **living stones** (Christians), those who have come to the ultimate **living stone** (Jesus).

i. This **spiritual house** shows that as much as Israel had a temple, Christians also have one. Yet the Christian's temple is **spiritual**, and they themselves are the temple.

ii. Jesus is first called the **living stone**; then we are called **living stones**. We live because we are connected with Him who is the source of life. "It is in union with him that they live, and answer the end of their regeneration; as stones of a building are of no use but as they occupy their proper places in a building, and rest on the foundation." (Clarke)

b. **Chosen by God and precious**: As much as God chose Israel, so the church is also **chosen**. As much as Israel had a priesthood, so Christians are a **holy priesthood**. And as much as Israel had sacrifices, so Christians **offer up spiritual sacrifices acceptable to God**.

i. **A holy priesthood**: The believer is his own priest before God. He does not need any mediator except his great High Priest, Jesus. "There can no longer be an elite priesthood with claims of special access to God, or special privileges in worship or in fellowship with God." (Grudem)

ii. Peter's idea isn't that God has abandoned Israel or that they have no place in His redemptive plan, but that Christianity is in no way inferior to Judaism.

c. **To offer up spiritual sacrifices acceptable to God through Jesus Christ**: God does the work of building (**being built**), but we do the job of offering sacrifices pleasing to Him, as we come to Jesus as who we are - **living stones**, made by Him.

i. Even a living stone cannot build something great for God as it sits all on its own. What God does in us *together* is important. He is building something out of us *together*.

ii. We can only serve as priests as we do it **through Jesus Christ**. In ourselves, we have no priestly authority, but only in Jesus.

3. (6-8) The glory of the Chief Cornerstone.

Therefore it is also contained in the Scripture, "Behold, I lay in Zion a chief cornerstone, elect, precious, and he who believes on Him will by no means be put to shame." Therefore, to you who believe, *He is* precious; but to those who are disobedient, "The stone which the builders rejected has become the chief cornerstone," and "A stone of stumbling and a rock of offense." They stumble, being disobedient to the word, to which they also were appointed.

a. **Behold, I lay in Zion a chief cornerstone**: If we are being built into a *spiritual house*, there is no doubt who our **Chief Cornerstone** is. Even though men **rejected** Jesus, He has become the **Chief Cornerstone** in the work of building the church.

i. Jesus Christ is the cornerstone of Psalm 118, the stumbling stone of Isaiah 8, the foundation stone of Isaiah 28, the supernatural stone of Daniel 2, and the rock that miraculously gave Israel water in the wilderness (1 Corinthians 10:4).

b. **Therefore, to you who believe, He is precious**: Though this **chief cornerstone** is rejected by the **disobedient** and unbelieving, undeniably **He is precious** to those who **believe**. One way to know if a person has truly Biblical faith is to see if Jesus is truly **precious** to them.

i. When Charles Spurgeon was 16 years old, he preached his first sermon in a village cottage to a handful of poor people, and he chose for his text 1 Peter 2:7: "*Unto you therefore which believe He is precious.*" Spurgeon said that he didn't think he could have preached on any other Bible passage, "but Christ was precious to my soul and I was in the flush of my youthful love, and I could not be silent when a precious Jesus was the subject." (Spurgeon)

ii. "Is Jesus precious to your soul? Remember, on your answer to this question depends your condition. You believe, if he is precious to you, but if he is not precious, then you are not believers, and you are condemned already because you believe not on the Son of God." (Spurgeon)

- Christ is precious *intrinsically.*
- Christ is precious *positively.*
- Christ is precious *comparatively.*
- Christ is precious *superlatively.*
- Christ is precious *suitably* to the need of the believer.

iii. This is true; though G. Campbell Morgan preferred the Revised Version translation: *For you therefore which believe is the preciousness.* "The declaration is not that believers know the preciousness of Christ; it is rather that they share it. . . . The qualities of Christ that create His preciousness, His honour, are placed at the disposal of the believer."

iv. "*The honour is to you who believe*; *i.e.* the honour of being in this building, and of having your souls saved through the blood of the Lamb, and becoming sons and daughters of God Almighty." (Clarke)

c. **The stone which the builders rejected Has become the chief cornerstone**: Those who reject the Chief Cornerstone and refuse to build on Him instead **stumble** over Him. Instead of being their salvation, Jesus becomes to them **a rock of offense**.

i. Jesus quoted this passage from Psalm 118 in regard to Himself (Matthew 21:42). A **chief cornerstone** is the starting point of a building; everything is laid out according to its connection to the **chief cornerstone**. Because it stands at the *corner*, the same stone is the starting place for two walls.

ii. Thus Jesus set out the course for both Jew and Gentile to be joined together into one glorious house for God. This in itself was **a stone of stumbling and a rock of offense** for the Jews, who thought that Gentiles should not have equal share with the Jews into God's great house.

iii. In the thinking of many Jews of that time, God should not have built a new building with both Jew and Gentile. He should have simply renovated the present structure of Judaism (adding Jesus as the Messiah) and invited Gentiles to come into that structure. But God did something different, and it was **a stone of stumbling and a rock of offense** for many first-century Jews.

iv. Therefore these great titles of 1 Peter 2:9-10 now apply to *all* believers, Jew and Gentile alike; whereas before they only applied to the Jewish people as God's covenant people.

d. **They stumble, being disobedient to the word, to which they also were appointed**: It is **appointed** that those who are **disobedient to the word** should stumble over Jesus.

i. When Jesus spoke of Himself as the **stone** of Psalm 118, He spoke of what those who rejected Him are **appointed** to: "*And whoever falls on this stone will be broken; but on whomever it falls, it will grind him to powder.*" (Matthew 21:44)

4. (9-10) The privileged place of God's people.

But you *are* a chosen generation, a royal priesthood, a holy nation, His own special people, that you may proclaim the praises of Him who called you out of darkness into His marvelous light; who once *were* not a people but *are* now the people of God, who had not obtained mercy but now have obtained mercy.

a. **But you are a chosen generation**: The things that once exclusively belonged to Israel - their election (**chosen**), **priesthood**, and calling are now no longer the property of Israel alone. These are now the property of every Christian, and we have them in a greater and spiritual sense.

i. We are **a royal priesthood**. The offices of *royalty* and **priesthood** were jealously separated in Israel. But Jesus, who is our King and Priest, has brought them together for His people.

b. **His own special people**: We are **special** because we belong to God. A museum may be filled with quite ordinary things: hats, canes, shoes, and so forth; but they may be significant because they once belonged to someone famous. God takes ordinary people; and because He works in them, they are **special**.

i. These same titles were applied to Israel (Exodus 19:5-6, Deuteronomy 4:20, Deuteronomy 7:6, and Isaiah 43:20-21). Now in Jesus we belong to God as **His own special people**.

ii. "The description of the Church is systematic and exhaustive. It is a race, and this suggests its life principle. It is a priesthood, and so has right of access to God. It is a nation, and so is under His government. It is a possession, and so is actually indwelt by Him." (Morgan)

c. **Who once were not a people but are now the people of God**: We once were without these privileges, and were not even **a people** before God. We had not seen the mercy of God, but **now have obtained mercy**.

i. In our culture, with its Christian foundations, we don't easily understand the great sense of privilege and relief that came to Gentiles as they were shared in the New Covenant with the God of Israel. Peter's message is wonderful: "You didn't used to belong, but now you belong to God and among God's people."

d. **That you may proclaim the praises of Him who called you out of darkness into His marvelous light**: The purpose for these high privileges is not so we can grow proud, but so that we can **proclaim the praises of Him** who has done such great things for us.

i. Since it is true that believers have a new life principle (**chosen generation**), a new access to God (**royal priesthood**), a new government (**holy nation**), and a new owner (**His own special people**), it will affect the way the believer lives life. That effect is described in the following verses.

B. How those who have come to Jesus are to live.

1. (11-12) When we come to Jesus, we are to abstain from fleshly lusts.

Beloved, I beg *you* as sojourners and pilgrims, abstain from fleshly lusts which war against the soul, having your conduct honorable among the Gentiles, that when they speak against you as evildoers, they may, by *your* good works which they observe, glorify God in the day of visitation.

a. **Abstain from fleshly lusts**: We can only **abstain from fleshly lusts** as we live **as sojourners and pilgrims**, as those who recognize that this world is not their home, and that they have a home and a citizenship in heaven.

b. **Which war against the soul**: Peter understands that these **fleshly lusts . . . *war* against the soul**. To be a Christian means to fight against the lusts of the flesh, and the battle continues as long as we live in this flesh.

i. It is easy to see how the pursuit of fleshly lusts can destroy our physical body. Just ask the alcoholic dying of liver disease, or ask the sexually immoral person with AIDS or one of the 350,000 people on this earth who contracted a sexually transmitted disease in the last 24 hours. But Peter reminds us that fleshly lusts also **war against the *soul***. Some escape disease in the physical body when they sin, but the disease and death of the inner man is a penalty that no one given over to the flesh escapes.

c. **Having your conduct honorable among the Gentiles**: This kind of godly living makes our conduct **honorable among** those who don't know God yet. Though we can expect that they will **speak against you as evildoers**, they can still be brought to **glorify God** by seeing our godly conduct.

i. Christians were falsely accused of great crimes in the early church. Pagans said that at communion Christians ate the flesh and drank the blood of a baby in a cannibalistic ritual. They said that Christian "agape feasts" were wild orgies. They said that Christians were antisocial because they did not participate in society's immoral entertainment. They said that Christians were atheists because they did not worship idols.

ii. But over time, it was clear that Christians were not immoral people - and it was shown by their lives. "The striking fact of history is that by their lives the Christians actually did defeat the slanders of the heathen. In the early part of the third century Celsus made the most famous and the most systematic attack of all upon the Christians in which he accused them of ignorance and foolishness and superstition and all kinds of things - *but never of immorality.*" (Barclay)

d. **The day of visitation**: This is probably a reference to their ultimate meeting with God, either when they go to meet Him or when He comes to meet them. The idea is that **the Gentiles** might be persuaded to become Christians by seeing the lives of other Christians, and that they would **glorify God** when they meet Him instead of cowering before His holy judgment.

i. "That the *day of visitation* means a time in which punishment should be inflicted, is plain from Isaiah 10:3: *And what will ye do in the* DAY *of* VISITATION, *and in the desolation which shall come from afar? To whom will ye flee for help? And where will ye leave your glory?*" (Clarke)

2. (13-17) When we come to Jesus, we are to show proper submission to the government.

Therefore submit yourselves to every ordinance of man for the Lord's sake, whether to the king as supreme, or to governors, as to those who are sent by him for the punishment of evildoers and *for the* praise of those who do good. For this is the will of God, that by doing good you may put to silence the ignorance of foolish men; as free, yet not using liberty as a cloak for vice, but as bondservants of God. Honor all *people.* Love the brotherhood. Fear God. Honor the king.

a. **Therefore submit yourselves to every ordinance of man**: As Christians we should be good citizens, submitting to government. This was very different from those zealous Jews in Peter's day who recognized no king but God and paid taxes to no one except God.

i. Peter wrote this in the days of the Roman Empire, which was not a democracy and no special friend to Christians. Yet he still recognized the legitimate authority of the Roman government.

ii. "The meaning of St. Peter appears to be this: the Jews thought it unlawful to obey any ruler that was not of *their own stock*; the apostle tells them that they should obey their civil magistrate, let him be of what stock he may, whether Jew or Gentile, and let him exercise the government in whatsoever *form*." (Clarke)

b. **For the Lord's sake**: This is why we obey the government. Since governments have a rightful authority from God, we are bound to obey them - unless, of course, they order us to do something in contradiction to God's law. Then, we are commanded to obey God before man (Acts 4:19).

> i. "God, as their supreme governor, shows them that it is his will that they should act uprightly and obediently at all times, and thus confound the ignorance of foolish men, who were ready enough to assert that their religion made them bad subjects." (Clarke)

c. **As to those who are sent by him**: Peter also insisted that *rulers* are **sent by him**; that is, **sent by** God. Governments are sent by God for the **punishment of evildoers** and for the recognition of those who do good.

> i. God uses governing authorities as a check upon man's sinful desires and tendencies. Governments are a useful tool in resisting the effects of man's fallen nature. Based also on what Paul wrote in Romans 13, we can say that the greatest offense government can make is to fail to punish evildoers, or to reward evildoers through corruption.

d. **That by doing good you may put to silence the ignorance of foolish men**: Peter knew that our conduct is a way to defend the gospel. He knew that those who never read the Bible will read our lives, so it is by **doing good** that we **put to silence the ignorance of foolish men**.

e. **Yet not using liberty as a cloak for vice, but as bondservants of God**: We are warned against taking the **liberty** we have in Jesus as an excuse for sin. Instead we use our **liberty** in Jesus to show the kind of love and respect that Peter calls for.

3. (18-20) When we come to Jesus, we are to show proper submission to our employers.

Servants, *be* submissive to *your* masters with all fear, not only to the good and gentle, but also to the harsh. For this *is* commendable, if because of conscience toward God one endures grief, suffering wrongfully. For what credit *is it* if, when you are beaten for your faults, you take it patiently? But when you do good and suffer, if you take it patiently, this *is* commendable before God.

> a. **Servants, be submissive to your masters**: The command to submit to masters isn't just to those who work for masters that are **good and gentle**, but also to those who are **harsh**. If we must endure hardship because of our Christian standards, it is then **commendable** before God.

b. **For what credit is it if, when you are beaten for your faults, you take it patiently?** To be punished for our wrongs is no **credit** to us. But when we are punished for doing good and endure it **patiently**, we are complimented **before God**.

> i. "It appears from this that the poor Christians, and especially those who had been converted to Christianity in a state of slavery, were often grievously abused; they were *buffeted* because they were Christians, and because they would not join with their masters in idolatrous worship." (Clarke)

> ii. "Our case is like that of a criminal who had better bear quietly a sentence for a crime he has not committed, lest by too much outcry he induce investigation into a list of offenses, which are not charged against him, because they are not known." (Meyer)

4. (21-25) The example of Jesus.

For to this you were called, because Christ also suffered for us, leaving us an example, that you should follow His steps: "Who committed no sin, nor was deceit found in His mouth"; who, when He was reviled, did not revile in return; when He suffered, He did not threaten, but committed *Himself* to Him who judges righteously; who Himself bore our sins in His own body on the tree, that we, having died to sins, might live for righteousness; by whose stripes you were healed. For you were like sheep going astray, but have now returned to the Shepherd and Overseer of your souls.

a. **Christ also suffered for us, leaving us an example**: Jesus is our **example** as someone who endured punishment unjustly. When **He was reviled** Jesus **did not revile in return**, but in His sufferings He **committed Himself** to the Father.

> i. "He suffered, but not on account of any evil he had either *done* or *said*. In *deed* and *word* he was immaculate, and yet he was exposed to suffering; expect the same, and when it comes bear it in the same spirit." (Clarke)

> ii. "Which hour do you think of the sufferings of the Lord, from Gethsemane to Golgotha, would be most deeply engraved upon the memory of Peter? Surely it would be that space of time in which he was mocked and buffeted in the hall of the high priest, when Peter sat and warmed his hands at the fire, when he saw his Lord abused, and was afraid to own that he was his disciple, and by-and-by became so terrified that, with profane language, he declared 'I know not the man.' So long as life lingered, the apostle would remember the meek and quiet bearing of his suffering Lord." (Spurgeon)

b. **Who Himself bore our sins in His own body on the tree**: The suffering of Jesus is clearly an example for us; but it is far more than an example. He also **bore our sins** as sin-bearing substitute, and provided for our healing (**by whose stripes you were healed**).

> i. Peter clearly meant the cross of Jesus when he mentioned the **tree** (literally *wood*). Jesus **bore our sins in His own body on the** *wood* - the wood of the cross. Peter stated it here both to constantly remind Christians of the great work of Jesus on the cross, *and* to show them that even as the suffering of Jesus accomplished much, so their own suffering can be used of God.

c. **That we, having died to sins, might live for righteousness**: Peter reminds us that when Jesus died on the cross, *we also* **died to sins**. Our life is permanently changed by our identification with Jesus on the cross, even as the Apostle Paul described in Romans 6.

> i. We have **died to sins** in the sense that our debt of sin and guilt was paid by Jesus' sacrifice on the cross. When we **died to sins** with Jesus on the cross, it means that He paid our debts. We do not trouble ourselves over debts that are paid. "He who bore my sins in his own body on the tree, took all my debts and paid them for me, and now I am dead to those debts; they have no power over me. I am dead to my sins; Christ suffered instead of me. I have nothing to do with them. They are gone as much as if they had never been committed." (Spurgeon)

> ii. We have **died to sins** in the sense that now a greater passion fills our life - a passion for the Lord Jesus Christ that is greater than our previous passion for sin. A miser may be dead to many pleasures and allurements of this world; but he is *alive* to the love of money. So we should be dead to sin but alive to Jesus.

d. **By whose stripes you were healed**: Peter quotes Isaiah 53:5, which primarily refers to spiritual healing but also includes physical healing. The provision for our healing (both physically and spiritually) is made by the sufferings (**stripes**) of Jesus. The physical aspect of our healing is received in part now, but only completely with our resurrection.

> i. In context we see that Peter's main point is that if a master treats us unjustly, we should not fear whatever harm he causes. We can be healed and restored by Jesus' suffering for us.

e. **For you were like sheep going astray, but have now returned to the Shepherd and Overseer of your souls**: If not for Jesus' patient endurance under the persecution of the ungodly, we would still be **going astray**. But because of His work for us, we have **returned** to the **Shepherd** (pastor) and the **Overseer** (bishop) of our souls.

1 Peter 3 - Submission and Suffering

A. Submission in the home.

1. (1-2) The heart of a godly wife.

Wives, likewise, *be* submissive to your own husbands, that even if some do not obey the word, they, without a word, may be won by the conduct of their wives, when they observe your chaste conduct *accompanied* by fear.

a. **Wives, likewise, be submissive to your own husbands**: The godly wife will **be submissive** to her husband. This submission isn't a reward for the husband's good behavior; as the proper order of the home, God commands it.

i. The teaching about submission was especially relevant to a first century married woman who had begun to follow Jesus. She would ask questions such as "Should I leave my husband?" or "Should I change my behavior towards him?" or "Should I assume a superior position to him because now I am in Jesus?"

ii. In the culture of the ancient world it was almost unthinkable for a wife to adopt a different religion than her husband. Christian women who came to Jesus before their husbands needed instruction.

b. **Likewise**: Proper submission in the home follows the same principles of submission as towards government or our employers. It is submission not only of the actions, but also of the heart - as demonstrated by the surrendering heart of Jesus (1 Peter 2:21-25).

i. The call for submission is not merely a call for love and considerate action. It is a call to take the place of submission to authority. The ancient Greek word translated *submission* was used outside the New Testament to describe the submission and obedience of soldiers in an army to those of superior rank. It literally means, "to order under."

ii. Yet submission to authority can be totally consistent with *equality* in importance, dignity, and honor. Jesus was subject to both His parents and to God the Father but was not lower than either of them. "Thus the command to wives to be subject to their husbands should never be taken to imply inferior personhood or spirituality, or lesser importance." (Grudem)

iii. Of course, submission in marriage follows the same principles as submission in other spheres. We submit to God appointed authority as our obligation before God, unless that authority directs us to sin. In that case it is right to obey God rather than men (Acts 4:19-20).

c. **Be submissive to your own husbands**: Peter carefully observed that wives are called to submit to their **own husbands** and not to all men in a general sense. Male headship is God's commanded principle for the home and the church, not for society in general.

i. The principle of submission is presented in many different ways in the New Testament.

- Jesus submitted to His parents (Luke 2:51).
- Demons submitted to the disciples (Luke 10:17).
- Citizens should submit to government authority (Romans 13:1 and 5, Titus 3:1, 1 Peter 2:13).
- The universe will submit to Jesus (1 Corinthians 15:27 and Ephesians 1:22).
- Unseen spiritual beings submit to Jesus (1 Peter 3:22).
- Christians should submit to their church leaders (1 Corinthians 16:15-16 and 1 Peter 5:5).
- Wives should submit to husbands (Colossians 3:18, Titus 2:5, 1 Peter 3:5, and Ephesians 5:22-24).
- The church should submit to Jesus (Ephesians 5:24).
- Servants should submit to masters (Titus 2:9, 1 Peter 2:18).
- Christians should submit to God (Hebrews 12:9, James 4:7).

ii. None of these relations are reversed. For example, masters are never told to submit to servants, Jesus is never told to submit to the church, and so forth. So while there must be a servant-like love and attitude on the part of those in positions of authority, that does not eliminate the concept of God's order of authority and the corresponding submission.

d. **That even if some do not obey the word, they, without a word, may be won by the conduct of their wives**: The benefit of submission is shown in the way that it affects husbands for God. A wife's submission is a powerful expression of her trust in God. This kind of faith and obedience can accomplish great things, even **without a word**.

i. Wives may want to shape their husbands, either guiding them to Jesus or guiding them in Jesus through their *words*. Peter reminds them that God's plan is that wives impact their husbands not through persuasive lectures, but through godly submission, **chaste conduct**, and the **fear** of God.

ii. There is a sense in which a wife's efforts to shape her husband through her own words and efforts may hinder the power of God's working on the husband. It is much more effective to submit in the way God says to, thus demonstrating trust in Him, and to let *God* have his way with the husband.

iii. "The attractiveness of a wife's submissive behaviour even to an unbelieving husband suggests that God has inscribed the rightness and beauty of role distinctions to include male leadership or headship in the family and female acceptance of and responsiveness to that leadership . . . The unbelieving husband sees this behaviour and deep within perceives the beauty of it. Within his heart there is a witness that this is right, this is how God intended men and women to relate as husband as wife. He concludes, therefore, that the gospel which his wife believes must be true as well." (Grudem)

e. **Do not obey the word**: This refers to an unbelieving husband, but it is a stronger idea than merely "do not believe." It has the idea of someone in active disobedience to God's word. Even *these* husbands can be won through the godly conduct of loving wives.

2. (3-4) The true beauty of a godly woman.

Do not let your adornment be *merely* outward; arranging the hair, wearing gold, or putting on *fine* apparel; rather *let it be* the hidden person of the heart, with the incorruptible *beauty* of a gentle and quiet spirit, which is very precious in the sight of God.

a. **Do not let your adornment be merely outward**: Peter did not forbid all **adornment**. But for the godly woman **outward** adornment is always in moderation, and her emphasis is always on *inward* adornment.

i. **Arranging the hair**: According to William Barclay, in the world Peter lived women often arranged and dyed their hair. They also wore wigs, especially blonde wigs made with hair imported from Germany. Peter had this in mind speaking of the **adornment** that is **merely outward**. Peter did not forbid a woman fixing her hair, or wearing jewelry, any more than he forbade her wearing **apparel** (*fine* is not in the original).

b. **Rather let it be the hidden person of the heart**: Real beauty comes from the **hidden person of the heart**. It isn't something you wear or primp before a mirror to have. It is something you *are*.

i. The real question is "What do you depend on to make yourself beautiful?" Peter's point is not that any of these are forbidden, but that they should not be a woman's **adornment**, the source of her true beauty.

c. **The incorruptible beauty of a gentle and quiet spirit**: The inner beauty of a godly woman is **incorruptible**. This means that it does not decay or get worse with age. Instead, **incorruptible beauty** only gets better with age, and is therefore of much greater value than the beauty that comes from the hair, jewelry, or clothing.

d. **A gentle and quiet spirit, which is very precious in the sight of God**: Peter described the character of true beauty - **a gentle and quiet spirit**. These character traits are not promoted for women by our culture; yet they are **very precious in the sight of God**.

3. (5-6) Examples of submission.

For in this manner, in former times, the holy women who trusted in God also adorned themselves, being submissive to their own husbands, as Sarah obeyed Abraham, calling him lord, whose daughters you are if you do good and are not afraid with any terror.

a. **In former times, the holy women who trusted in God also adorned themselves**: Peter reminds women that he did not call them to a new standard; but to something that was practiced by **holy women of former times**.

b. **Who trusted in God**: When women submit to their husbands and when they do not put trust in their outward adornment, they are like the holy women of former times who **trusted in God**. They powerfully demonstrate their faith.

i. A woman can trust her own ability to influence and control her husband, or she can trust God and *be submissive*. A woman can trust her outward beauty and adornment, or she can trust God and cultivate *a gentle and quiet spirit*. It all comes back to trust in God; so she should be like **the holy women who trusted in God**.

c. **As Sarah obeyed Abraham**: Two things demonstrated Sarah's submission to Abraham. First, she **obeyed** Abraham even when it was difficult and even when he was wrong (as in Genesis 12:10-20). Second, she *honored* Abraham by **calling him lord**. It is possible to *obey* someone without showing them the *honor* that is part of submission. True submission knows the place of both *obedience* and *honor*.

i. "An attitude of submission to a husband's authority will be reflected in numerous words and actions each day which reflect deference to his leadership and an acknowledgment of his final responsibility." (Grudem)

d. **If you do good and are not afraid with any terror**: True submission, full of faith in God has no room for fear or terror. It does good and leaves the result to God and not to man.

i. The words "**do good**" remind us that true submission is not a sulking surrender to authority. It is an active embrace of God's will, demonstrating trust in Him.

4. (7) The heart of a godly husband.

Husbands, likewise, dwell with *them* with understanding, giving honor to the wife, as to the weaker vessel, and as *being* heirs together of the grace of life, that your prayers may not be hindered.

a. **Dwell with them**: A godly husband lives with his wife. He doesn't merely share a house, but he truly *lives with* her. He recognizes the great point of Paul's teaching on marriage in Ephesians 5: that "*husbands ought to love their own wives as their own bodies; he who loves his wife loves himself*" (Ephesians 5:28). The godly husband understands the *essential unity* or *oneness* God has established between husband and wife.

b. **With understanding**: A godly husband undertakes the important job of **understanding** his wife. By knowing her well, he is able to demonstrate his love for her far more effectively.

i. When a husband has this **understanding**, God directs him to use it in that he is to **dwell with** his wife **with understanding**. He is supposed to take his **understanding** and apply it in daily life with his wife. This is where many men have trouble following through. They may *have* **understanding** about their wives, but they don't *use* it as they **dwell with them**.

c. **Giving honor**: A godly husband knows how to make his wife feel honored. Though she submits to him, he takes care that she does not feel like she is an employee or under a tyrant.

i. In **giving honor to the wife**, the word in the ancient Greek language for **the wife** is a rare word, meaning more literally "the feminine one." It suggests that the woman's feminine nature should prompt the husband to honor her.

ii. This was a *radical* teaching in the world Peter lived in. In that ancient culture a husband had absolute rights over his wife and the wife had virtually no rights in the marriage. In the Roman world, if a man caught his wife in an act of adultery he could kill her on the spot. But if a wife caught her husband, she could do nothing against him. All the duties and obligations in marriage were put on the wife. Peter's radical teaching is that the *husband* has God-ordained duties and obligations toward his wife.

d. **As to the weaker vessel**: In this context **weaker** speaks of the woman's relative physical weakness in comparison to men. Men aren't necessarily stronger spiritually than women, but they are generally stronger physically. As Peter brought in the idea of the woman's feminine nature with the words **the wife**, he continues in appreciating the feminine nature and how a husband should respond to it.

i. Therefore, a godly husband recognizes whatever limitations his wife has physically and he does not expect more from her than is appropriate and kind.

e. **Heirs together**: A godly husband realizes that his spouse is not only his wife, but also his sister in Jesus. Part of their inheritance in the Lord is only realized in their oneness as husband and wife.

i. **Heirs together**: This "reminds husbands that even though they have been given great authority within marriage, their wives are still equal to them in spiritual privilege and eternal importance: they are 'joint heirs.'" (Grudem)

f. **That your prayers may not be hindered**: The failure to live as a godly husband has spiritual consequences. It can and it will hinder prayer.

i. Some have thought that Peter has in mind here the **prayers** that husbands and wives pray together. But since he addresses husbands only, and because he says *your* **prayers**, he refers to the prayers of husbands in general.

ii. Peter *assumed* that the fear of **hindered** prayer would motivate Christian husbands to love and care for their wives as they should. Many Christian men have such a low regard for prayer that this warning may not adequately motivate them.

iii. "Indeed, to true believers prayer is so invaluable that the danger of hindering it is used by Peter as a motive why, in their marriage relationships, and household concerns, they should behave themselves with great wisdom. He bids the husband 'dwell' with his wife 'according to knowledge,' and render loving honor to her, lest their united prayers should be hindered. Anything which hinders prayer must be wrong. If any management of the family, or want of management, is injuring our power in prayer, there is an urgent demand for an alteration." (Spurgeon)

B. Godliness in suffering.

1. (8-9) A plea for unity and love among God's people.

Finally, all *of you be* of one mind, having compassion for one another; love as brothers, *be* tenderhearted, *be* courteous; not returning evil for

evil or reviling for reviling, but on the contrary blessing, knowing that you were called to this, that you may inherit a blessing.

a. **Be of one mind**: Most of us are willing to have **one mind**, as long as that **one mind** is *my mind!* But the **one mind** is to be *the mind of Christ* (1 Corinthians 2:16). Our common **mind** is to be Jesus' mind.

i. This command brings us back to the need to know God's word. We can't **be of one mind**, the mind of Jesus, if we don't know what His mind is. The word of God shows us the mind of Jesus.

b. **Be of one mind**: This speaks to the essential *unity* of God's people. We are one; but we are not all the same. While we should all **be of one mind**, we can't expect everyone to be like us. God has built both unity and diversity among His people.

i. Every cell of your body is different, and each one has its role to play. But every cell in your body has the same DNA code written in it, the master plan for the whole body. Every cell in your body has the same "mind."

ii. We could say that Christians should be like a good choir. Each one sings with his own voice and some sing different parts, but everyone sings to the same music and in harmony with one another.

c. **Having compassion . . . tenderhearted . . . courteous**: Peter described the kind of warm love that should be among the people of God. We should be compassionate, brotherly, tenderhearted, and even polite.

i. Remember that this was the measure Jesus gave to the world to identify His true disciples: "*By this all will know that you are My disciples, if you have love for one another*" (John 13:35). Jesus did not command us to *like* our brothers and sisters in Christ. But we are commanded to love them; and once we start loving them we will start liking them.

d. **Not returning evil for evil or reviling for reviling, but on the contrary blessing**: The greatest challenge to our love for others comes when we are wronged. At those times we are called to not return **evil for evil**, but to give a **blessing** instead.

i. No dispute, argument, or personality conflict among believers should linger. Even if one Christian gets out of line, the loving response of other Christians should keep the problem small and short-lived.

ii. The natural response to hostility is retaliation. This is what the terrible ethnic conflicts all over the world are all about - one group wrongs another, and dedicates the rest of its existence to repaying that wrong. Only the love of Jesus for our enemies can break the terrible cycle.

iii. Jesus reminded us that it is no great credit if we love those who love us in return; the real test of love is to demonstrate compassion to our enemies (Matthew 5:44-47).

e. **That you may inherit a blessing**: We love one another, but not only for the sake of Jesus, whose body we are members of. We love one another, but not only for the sake of our brother or sister for whom Jesus died. We also love one another for our *own sake* - by blessing those who have wronged us, we will **inherit a blessing**. If you can't love for the sake of Jesus, or for the sake of your brother, then do it for your *own sake*!

2. (10-12) A quotation from Psalm 34:12-16 demonstrates the blessing that comes to those who turn away from evil and do good.

For "He who would love life and see good days, let him refrain his tongue from evil, and his lips from speaking deceit. Let him turn away from evil and do good; let him seek peace and pursue it. For the eyes of the LORD *are* on the righteous, and His ears *are open* to their prayers; but the face of the LORD *is* against those who do evil."

a. **Let him turn away from evil and do good**: Doing good is often difficult because as a general rule, evil is rewarded immediately and the reward of doing good is often delayed. But the rewards of good are better and far more secure than the rewards of doing evil. God promises this in the passage quoted by Peter.

3. (13-17) How to handle it when our good is returned with evil.

And who *is* he who will harm you if you become followers of what is good? But even if you should suffer for righteousness' sake, *you are* blessed. "And do not be afraid of their threats, nor be troubled." But sanctify the Lord God in your hearts, and always *be* ready to *give* a defense to everyone who asks you a reason for the hope that is in you, with meekness and fear; having a good conscience, that when they defame you as evildoers, those who revile your good conduct in Christ may be ashamed. For *it is* better, if it is the will of God, to suffer for doing good than for doing evil.

a. **And who is he who will harm you**: Though Peter says that Christians should always answer evil with good, he also lived in the real world and he knew that people often repaid good with a response of evil.

i. "Not to be hated by the world; to be loved and flattered and caressed by the world - is one of the most terrible positions in which a Christian can find himself. 'What bad thing have I done,' asked the ancient sage, 'that he should speak well of me?' " (Meyer)

b. **If you become followers of what is good**: Literally, **become followers** is "be zealous." "*Some* Jews were zealots, boasting their zeal for the Lord or His Law . . . *all* Christians should be *zealots for that which is good.*" (Hart)

c. **But even if you should suffer for righteousness' sake, you are blessed**: Peter reminds us that there is even a blessing for us when we **suffer for righteousness' sake**. God will care for us, especially when we **suffer** unjustly.

> i. Jesus spoke of the same attitude: "*And do not fear those who kill the body but cannot kill the soul. But rather fear Him who is able to destroy both soul and body in hell*" (Matthew 10:28).

d. **And do not be afraid of their threats, nor be troubled**: The presence or possibility of suffering for doing good should not make us shrink back from doing good. Instead we should give a special place (**sanctify**) to God in our hearts, and always be ready to explain our faith (**give a defense**), always doing it with a right attitude (**meekness and fear**).

> i. Other manuscripts render **sanctify the Lord God in your hearts** as, *sanctify Christ as Lord in your hearts*. "The simple meaning of the injunction is that at the very centre of life there is to be one Lord, and that is Christ. . . . Other lords are permitted to invade the sanctuary of the heart, and to exercise dominion over us. Our own selfish desires, the opinion of others, worldly wisdom, the pressure of circumstances, these and many other lords command us, and we turn away our simple and complete allegiance to our one Lord." (Morgan)

> ii. We can **be ready to give a defense** if we have made ourselves ready in knowing the Bible. Peter knew how important it was to **give a defense to everyone who asks you**. He had to do this in the situations described in Acts 2:14-39, Acts 3:11-26, Acts 4:8-12, and Acts 5:29-32. In each point of testing Peter relied on the power of the Holy Spirit and was able to **give a defense**.

e. **Those who revile your good conduct in Christ may be ashamed**: Our **good conduct**, when our good is returned with evil, will prove others wrong in their opinions about us and it will make them **ashamed** for speaking against our godly lives.

f. **For it is better, if it is the will of God, to suffer for doing good than for doing evil**: None of us want to suffer. But if we must, may it be for **doing good** and not for **doing evil**. Sometimes Christians are obnoxious and offensive and are made **to suffer** for it. They may wish it were persecution for the sake of the gospel, but really it is simply suffering **for doing evil**.

C. Jesus shows the power of suffering for doing good.

1. (18) Through His godly suffering, Jesus brought us to God.

For Christ also suffered once for sins, the just for the unjust, that He might bring us to God, being put to death in the flesh but made alive by the Spirit,

a. **For Christ also suffered once for sins**: Jesus **suffered once for sins**. There is no longer any sacrifice or atonement that can please God other than what Jesus provided at the cross. Even our own suffering won't pay for our sins. The price has already been paid.

i. Though Peter used the suffering of Christ as an encouragement and strength to his afflicted readers, we must remember that Peter also set Jesus completely apart from all others in his suffering. Spurgeon recalled the heroic suffering of one godly man: "I remember reading, in Foxe's *Book of Martyrs,* the story of a man of God, who was bound to a stake to die for Christ; there he was, calm and quiet, till his legs had been burned away, and the bystanders looked to see his helpless body drop from the chains as black as coal, and not a feature could be discerned; but one who was near was greatly surprised to see that poor black carcass open its mouth, and two words came out of it; and what do you suppose they were? *'Sweet* Jesus!' And then the martyr fell over the chains, and at last life was gone."

ii. That saint had the sweet presence of Jesus to help him through his horrible suffering; but Jesus did not have the sweet presence of His Father to help Him on the cross. Instead, God the Father treated Him as if He were an enemy, as the target of the righteous wrath of God. In this sense, the suffering of Jesus on the cross was worse than any ever suffered by a martyr; perhaps not worse in the physical pain suffered, but certainly in the spiritual suffering and total experience.

iii. "It is almost as if the apostle said, 'You have none of you suffered when compared with him;' or, at least, he was the Arch-Sufferer, – the Prince of sufferers, - the Emperor of the realm of agony, - Lord Paramount in sorrow. . . . You know a little about grief, but you do not know much. The hem of grief's garment is all you ever touch, but Christ wore it as his daily robe. We do but sip of the cup he drank to its bitterest dregs. We feel just a little of the warmth of Nebuchadnezzar's furnace; but he dwelt in the very midst of the fire." (Spurgeon)

b. **The just for the unjust**: Jesus is a perfect example of suffering for doing good. He, the **just**, suffered for all of us who are **the unjust** - and the purpose of it all was to **bring us to God**, to restore our broken and dead relationship with Him.

i. Since Jesus did all this to **bring us to God**, how wrong it is for us to not come to God in fellowship! The ancient Greek word translated "**bring**" is the same word used for *access* in Romans 5:2 and Ephesians 2:18. In ancient literature, the word **bring** was used "of admission to an audience with the Great King." (Blum)

c. **Being put to death in the flesh but made alive by the Spirit**: Jesus did die in His body but was raised from the dead **by the** Holy **Spirit**. Here, the Bible tells us that the Holy Spirit raised Jesus from the dead. It also tells us that the Father raised Jesus from the dead (Romans 6:4), and it says that Jesus raised Himself from the dead (John 2:18-22). The resurrection was the work of the Triune God.

2. (19-20a) Through godly suffering, Jesus preached to the spirits in prison.

By whom also He went and preached to the spirits in prison, who formerly were disobedient,

a. **By whom**: This means that Jesus was *inspired by the Holy Spirit* when He did the work of preaching to the spirits in prison. He was *made alive by the Spirit*, and then also did this work by the same Spirit.

b. **He went and preached to the spirits in prison**: Apparently this work was done in the period after Jesus' death but before His first resurrection appearance to the disciples. Jesus went to Hades - the abode of the dead - and **preached to the spirits** there.

c. **Spirits in prison**: Though some have regarded these **spirits** as human spirits, it is more likely that they were demonic spirits. We know that their disobedience was *in the days of Noah* (1 Peter 3:20). We have evidence that this was a time of gross sin for both demons and humans, when there was an ungodly mingling of humans and demons (Genesis 6:1-2).

   i. "Apparently, the oldest identification of those imprisoned spirits understood them as the fallen angels of Genesis 6. That view was widely known and generally taken for granted in the apostolic era." (Hiebert)

d. **Preached to the spirits in prison**: We also don't know exactly why Jesus **preached** to these imprisoned spirits. In all probability this was *preaching* (the proclamation of God's message), but it was not *evangelism* (the proclamation of good news). Jesus **preached** a message of *judgment* and final condemnation in light of His finished work on the cross to these disobedient spirits.

   i. In doing this there was a completion in Jesus' triumph over evil, even the evil that happened before the flood. The Bible says that even those *under the earth* must acknowledge Jesus' ultimate Lordship. Here Jesus was announcing that fact: "*that at the name of Jesus every knee should bow, of those in heaven, and of those on earth, and of those under the earth*" (Philippians 2:10).

   ii. "We do not believe that Peter said that Christ preached the gospel to those imprisoned spirits; he taught that Christ announced His triumph over evil, which was bad news for them. For Peter's readers, however, it meant comfort and encouragement." (Hiebert)

iii. "What His message was we are not told. Why only those disobedient in the days of Noah are mentioned is not stated. What the purpose or result of Christ's preaching was, is not revealed. On all these points we may form our own conclusions, but we have no authority for anything approaching dogmatic teaching." (Morgan)

3. (20b-22) The salvation of Noah as a picture of baptism.

When once the Divine longsuffering waited in the days of Noah, while *the* **ark was being prepared, in which a few, that is, eight souls, were saved through water. There is also an antitype which now saves us; baptism (not the removal of the filth of the flesh, but the answer of a good conscience toward God), through the resurrection of Jesus Christ, who has gone into heaven and is at the right hand of God, angels and authorities and powers having been made subject to Him.**

a. **Eight souls, were saved through water**: Peter drew a picture with his words here. Even as Noah's salvation from the judgment of God was connected with **water**, so the Christian's salvation is connected with **water**, the water of **baptism**.

i. The water of the flood washed away sin and wickedness and brought a new world with a fresh start before God. The water of baptism does the same thing, providing a passage from the old to the new.

b. **Not the removal of the filth of the flesh, but the answer of a good conscience toward God**: At the same time Peter was careful to point out that it isn't the actual water washing of baptism that saves us, but the spiritual reality behind the immersion in water. What really saves us is the **answer of a good conscience toward God**, a conscience made **good** through the completed work of Jesus.

c. **Christ, who has gone into heaven and is at the right hand of God**: We see the completeness of Jesus' work by His exaltation to the **right hand of God** the Father, and the subjection of all created spirits unto Him (**angels and authorities and powers having been made subject to Him**). So though Jesus suffered for doing good, He had the ultimate triumph. The example of Jesus proves Peter's point in 1 Peter 3:9: when we suffer for doing good, we will inherit a blessing.

i. Jesus **has gone into heaven**, and it is better for us that He is there. Spurgeon related this to how the high priest, ministering for Israel on the Day of Atonement, disappeared from the people and went behind the veil. "Though he was not with them, he was with God, which was better for them. The high priest was more useful to them within the veil than outside of it; he was doing for them out of sight what he could not accomplish in their view. I delight to think that my Lord is with the Father. Sometimes I cannot get to God, my access seems blocked by my infirmity; but he is always with God to plead for me."

ii. Our connection with Jesus is like the little boy with his kite. His kite flew so high in the sky that he could no longer see it. Someone asked him, "How do you know it is still up there?" The boy answered, "I can feel it pull." We can't see Jesus enthroned in heaven, but we can certainly feel Him pull us toward Himself.

iii. Since Jesus **has gone into heaven**, His Church is safe. "Let not his church tremble, let her not think of putting out the hand of unbelief to steady the ark of the Lord. The history of the church is to be the history of Christ repeated: she is to be betrayed, she is to be scourged, she is to be falsely accused and spitted on; she may have her crucifixion and her death; but she shall rise again. Her Master rose, and like him she shall rise and receive glory. You can never kill the church till you can kill Christ; and you can never defeat her till you defeat the Lord Jesus, who already wears the crown of triumph." (Spurgeon)

1 Peter 4 - Serving God in the Last Days

A. Attitudes for end-times believers.

1. (1-2) In the last days, Christians should have an attitude of commitment.

Therefore, since Christ suffered for us in the flesh, arm yourselves also with the same mind, for he who has suffered in the flesh has ceased from sin, that he no longer should live the rest of *his* time in the flesh for the lusts of men, but for the will of God.

a. **Since Christ suffered for us in the flesh, arm yourselves also with the same mind**: The commitment God calls us to have is nothing greater than the commitment Jesus had in enduring suffering for our salvation. In the last days we need to have a commitment to God that will endure through great struggles.

i. Jesus communicated the same idea when He told us that anyone who would come after Him must take up his cross and follow (Matthew 16:24). Taking up the cross meant that you were absolutely committed and not looking back.

ii. **Arm yourself with the same mind**: Many of us are defeated in our battle against sin because we refuse to sacrifice anything in the battle. We only want victory if it comes easily to us. Jesus called us to have the kind of attitude that would sacrifice in the battle against sin (Matthew 5:29-30).

b. **He who has suffered in the flesh has ceased from sin**: When a person suffers physical persecution for the sake of Jesus, it almost always profoundly changes their outlook regarding sin and the pursuit of the lusts of the flesh. That one is more likely to **live the rest of his time in the flesh** not **for the lusts of men, but for the will of God**.

i. "Whoever has suffered for doing right, and has still gone on obeying God in spite of the suffering it involved, has made a clear break with sin." (Grudem)

ii. Hiebert observes that the phrase **has ceased from sin** "Depicts the spiritual state of the victorious sufferer. It carries a note of triumph; he has effectively broken with a life dominated by sin. It need not mean that he no longer commits any act of sin, but that his old life, dominated by the power of sin, has been terminated."

iii. If we have not physically suffered for following Jesus Christ, we can still connect ourselves by faith to Jesus, who has **suffered for us in the flesh**. "I beg you to remember that there is no getting quit of sin – there is no escaping from its power – except by contact and union with the Lord Jesus Christ." (Spurgeon)

c. **He no longer should live the rest of his time**: Peter gave us two time references that are helpful in having the right attitude in our following of Jesus Christ.

- First, **no longer** should we live in sin, and we should answer every temptation and sinful impulse with the reply, "**no longer**."

- Second, we should carefully consider how to **live the rest of** our **time**. God has appointed us some further days on this earth; when each of us must answer to Him how we **live** this **time**.

2. (3-6) In the last days, Christians should live with an attitude of wisdom.

For we *have spent* enough of our past lifetime in doing the will of the Gentiles; when we walked in lewdness, lusts, drunkenness, revelries, drinking parties, and abominable idolatries. In regard to these, they think it strange that you do not run with *them* in the same flood of dissipation, speaking evil of *you*. They will give an account to Him who is ready to judge the living and the dead. For this reason the gospel was preached also to those who are dead, that they might be judged according to men in the flesh, but live according to God in the spirit.

a. **For we have spent enough of our past lifetime in doing the will of the Gentiles**: Peter realized we have all spent enough time living like the world. Now we are called to live like Christians. It is a profound and foolish waste of time for Christians to live like the world, and we must simply stop being double-minded and start living as Christians.

i. Sadly, many Christians (in their heart of hearts) think that they have *not* **spent enough** time doing the will of the ungodly. They want to experience more of the world before they make a full commitment to godliness. This is a tragic mistake and takes a path that leads *away* from eternal life.

b. **Lewdness**: This word begins a list of sins that Peter understood should only mark the *past* life of Christians and not the present. This word means to live without any sense of moral restraint, especially in regard to sexual immorality and violence.

i. **Lewdness** "denotes excesses of all kinds of evil. Involving a lack of personal self-restraint, the term pictures sin as an inordinate indulgence of appetites to the extent of violating a sense of public decency." (Hiebert)

ii. When we look at this list (**lewdness, lusts, drunkenness, revelries, drinking parties, and abominable idolatries**), we see just how little fallen man has progressed in the last 2,000 years. These problems have not been solved in the time since Peter wrote this letter.

c. **They think it strange that you do not run with them in the same flood of dissipation**: When the world looks at our godly living, they **think it strange** that we do not follow them in their **flood of dissipation** (wastefulness). If life lived after the flesh is anything, it is a *waste*.

i. **Speaking evil of you**: When we don't participate in the sin around us, we convict those who practice their sin, and they don't like that - so they speak evil of us.

ii. "It does not matter how your good deeds are received by men. If you are like God, you will find them received with contempt and ingratitude." (Meyer)

iii. "Since heathen religious ceremonies were part and parcel of ordinary life (e.g., all civic and national activities were bound up with them) the Christians were compelled to avoid what would have seemed to their fellows a wholly innocuous co-operation and to go much further than merely separate themselves from actual heathen worship." (Best, cited in Hiebert)

d. **They will give an account to Him who is ready to judge**: When this account is required, all who live in the sins Peter described will clearly see how foolish they have been. Even if one seems to live the "good life" living by the world's rules, his life will be a waste in the measure of eternity.

e. **For this reason the gospel was preached also to those who are dead**: Peter also says that because of this eternal judgment the gospel was preached to the **dead**. The righteous **dead** know and live on in constant awareness of the reality of eternity - and are rewarded by this understanding as they **live according to God in the spirit**.

i. Peter has already told us that Jesus preached to the *spirits in prison*, preaching a message of judgment (1 Peter 3:19). Apparently during this same time Jesus also preached a message of salvation to the faithful dead in Abraham's Bosom (Luke 16:22) who anticipated the work of the Messiah for them. This preaching **to those who are dead** was not the offer of a second chance, but the completion of the salvation of those who had been faithful to God under their first chance.

ii. In doing this, Jesus fulfilled the promised that He would lead *captivity captive* (Psalm 68:18 and Ephesians 4:8) and He would "*proclaim liberty to the captives and the opening of the prison to those who are bound*" (Isaiah 61:1 and Luke 4:18).

iii. It may also be that Peter here had in mind those in the Christian community who had already died, perhaps even dying as martyrs. If this is the case then Peter used their heroic example as a way to encourage his suffering readers to also be faithful.

3. (7) In the last days, Christians should live with an attitude of serious prayer.

But the end of all things is at hand; therefore be serious and watchful in your prayers.

a. **The end of all things is at hand**: If we really believe that we live in the last days, it is all the more appropriate that we give ourselves to prayer (**therefore be serious and watchful in your prayers**).

i. "The assertion that the end of the age does indeed stand near and may break in at any time well represents the view of the early church." (Hiebert)

ii. Many Christians who believe that Jesus is coming soon based on prophecy charts and political events fail to apply that belief in the proper way. They fail to apply themselves to more diligent prayer.

b. **Therefore be serious . . . in your prayers**: We must give ourselves to **serious** prayer. As we see the weight of eternity rushing towards us, we dare not take the need for prayer lightly.

c. **Therefore be . . . watchful in your prayers**: We must give ourselves to **watchful** prayer, primarily having our hearts and minds watching and ready for the return of Jesus Christ. But this also means watching ourselves and watching this world, measuring our readiness for Jesus' coming.

4. (8-11) In the last days, Christians should live with an attitude of love.

And above all things have fervent love for one another, for "love will cover a multitude of sins." *Be* **hospitable to one another without grumbling. As each one has received a gift, minister it to one another, as good stewards of the manifold grace of God. If anyone speaks,** *let him speak* **as the oracles of God. If anyone ministers,** *let him do it* **as with the ability which God supplies, that in all things God may be glorified through Jesus Christ, to whom belong the glory and the dominion forever and ever. Amen.**

a. **Above all things have fervent love for one another**: If these are the last days, then it is important for us to love those we are going to spend eternity with. In light of eternity, we must have **fervent love for one another**.

b. **For "love will cover a multitude of sins"**: Love does **cover a multitude of sins**, both the sins of the one loving and the sins of the one who is being loved.

> i. "Where love abounds in a fellowship of Christians, many small offences, and even some large ones, are readily overlooked and forgotten. But where love is lacking, every word is viewed with suspicion, every action is liable to misunderstanding, and conflicts about - to Satan's perverse delight." (Grudem)

c. **Be hospitable to one another without grumbling**: Love will show itself in hospitality. Christians should often open their homes to others and doing it all **without grumbling**.

> i. " 'Without grumbling' is a frank recognition that the practice of hospitality could become costly, burdensome, and irritating. The Greek term denotes a muttering or low speaking as a sign of displeasure. It depicts a spirit that is the opposite of cheerfulness." (Hiebert)

d. **As each one has received a gift, minister it to one another**: Love will show itself as we give to the church family what God has given us as gifts. As we do so, we are **good stewards** of the many-faceted (**manifold**) **grace of God** given to us.

> i. In 1 Corinthians 15:10 Paul makes it clear that he was what he was only by God's grace. But at the same time, "*His grace toward me was not in vain*" because Paul put his own God-inspired efforts to work with God's grace. The idea is that if we are *bad* **stewards of the manifold grace of God**, it is as if that grace was given to us in vain. That grace is wasted, because it only comes *to* us and doesn't move *through* us.

> ii. "*Manifold grace* is many-coloured grace. As when a ray of light breaks into a spray of many hues, so each of us receives God's grace at a different angle, and flashes it back broken up into some fresh colour." (Meyer)

e. **If anyone ministers, let him do it as with the ability which God supplies**: Every part is important; each has its job to do. Even the smallest, seemingly least important part of the body of Christ is important.

> i. A man was rebuilding the engine to his lawn mower, and when he finished, he had one small part left over, and he couldn't remember where it went. He started the engine and it ran great, so he figured that the part was useless - until he tried to stop the lawn mower, and it wouldn't stop! Even the smallest, seemingly least important part of the body of Christ is important.

> ii. As we serve **one another**, we do it with the strength God provides, **the ability which God supplies** - so that to Him **belong the glory and the dominion forever and ever**.

B. Understanding your time of trial.

  1. (12-13) Enduring trials with the right attitude.

Beloved, do not think it strange concerning the fiery trial which is to try you, as though some strange thing happened to you; but rejoice to the extent that you partake of Christ's sufferings, that when His glory is revealed, you may also be glad with exceeding joy.

    a. **Concerning the fiery trial which is to try you**: Instead of thinking of trials (even **fiery** trials) as **strange** occurrences, we see them as ways to **partake of Christ's sufferings**. And if we partake of His sufferings, we will also partake of His **glory** and **joy**.

      i. Peter once told Jesus to avoid the suffering of the cross (Mark 8:32-33). "Once it seemed strange to the Apostle Peter that his Master should think of suffering. Now he thinks it strange that He could have imagined anything else." (Meyer)

    b. **Partake of Christ's sufferings**: We can only **partake** of Jesus' sufferings because He partook of our humanity and sufferings. He became a man and suffered so that our suffering wouldn't be meaningless. It is good to share *anything* with Jesus, even His suffering.

    c. **Rejoice to the extent that you partake of Christ's sufferings, that when His glory is revealed, you may also be glad with exceeding joy**: Our tendency is to embrace the glory and the joy and to avoid any sharing of Jesus' suffering. Or we morbidly fixate on the suffering and forget that it is but a necessary prelude to the **glory** and **joy**.

      i. We should never deny the place of suffering in building godliness in the Christian life. Though there is much needless pain we bear through lack of knowledge or faith, there is also necessary suffering. If suffering was a suitable tool to teach Jesus (Hebrews 5:8), it is a suitable tool to teach His servants.

      ii. **To the extent** implies a measure. Those who have suffered more in Jesus will rejoice more at His coming in **glory**.

  2. (14-16) The difference between suffering as a Christian and suffering as an evildoer.

If you are reproached for the name of Christ, blessed *are you,* for the Spirit of glory and of God rests upon you. On their part He is blasphemed, but on your part He is glorified. But let none of you suffer as a murderer, a thief, an evildoer, or as a busybody in other people's matters. Yet if *anyone suffers* as a Christian, let him not be ashamed, but let him glorify God in this matter.

a. **If you are reproached for the name of Christ**: Suffering for **the name of Christ** is a blessing, because it shows that we really are following Jesus, and that we suffer because we are identified with Him.

b. **On their part He is blasphemed, but on your part He is glorified**: We expect the world to blaspheme Jesus. But He should always be **glorified** among Christians.

c. **Let none of you suffer as a murderer, a thief, an evildoer, or as a busybody**: Suffering as **an evildoer** is deserved and brings shame to the name of Jesus. Peter recognized that not all suffering that Christians experience is suffering in **the name of Jesus**.

> i. We understand when Peter writes about the suffering that might come to the **murderer**, the **thief**, or the **evildoer**. Yet we shouldn't be surprised that he also includes the **busybody in other people's matters**. Such people *do* suffer a lot of grief and pain, but not for the sake of Jesus.

d. **If anyone suffers as a Christian, let him not be ashamed**: Suffering as a Christian is nothing to be ashamed about, even though the world may despise the suffering Christian. Instead, we should **glorify God** *in* these matters.

> i. We don't glorify God for suffering. But we do glorify Him **in** suffering, and we glorify Him for what He will accomplish in us and through us with the suffering.

> ii. "The name 'Christian' (*Christianos*), built on the name *Christ* with the suffix *–ianos*, a Latin formation (*-ianus*), denotes a partisan follower. . . . *Christian* categorized the followers of Christ as 'members of the Christ-party,' not 'little Christ' as some popular explanations would have it." (Hiebert)

> iii. Christians were first known as "disciples," "believers," "the Lord's disciples," or "those who belonged to the Way" before they were known as Christians, first at Acts 11:26. This is the first of three places in the New Testament where the followers of Jesus are named Christians.

> > • In Acts 11:26 it tells us *the disciples were first called Christians in Antioch.*

> > • In Acts 26:28 Agrippa told Paul, *You almost persuade me to become a Christian.* This shows that between Acts 11:26 and 26:28 **Christian** had become a popularized name for the followers of Jesus.

> > • In 1 Peter 4:16 the idea is that some are suffering because they are identified as Christians. This shows that the name had become very widely used, so much so that one could be persecuted for being numbered as a **Christian**.

3. (17-19) Committing your soul to God in the midst of suffering.

For the time *has come* for judgment to begin at the house of God; and if *it begins* with us first, what will *be* the end of those who do not obey the gospel of God? Now "If the righteous one is scarcely saved, where will the ungodly and the sinner appear?" Therefore let those who suffer according to the will of God commit their souls *to Him* in doing good, as to a faithful Creator.

    a. **For the time has come for judgment to begin at the house of God**: In the context of suffering, Peter tells us that judgment begins at the **house of God**. Right now, God uses suffering as a **judgment** (in a positive, purifying sense) for Christians (**the house of God**).

        i. It is *right* for judgment to begin at the house of God. "There is equity in it; for Christians profess to be better than others, and so they ought to be. They say they are regenerate, so they ought to be regenerate. They say that they are a holy people, separated unto Christ; so they ought to be holy, and separate from sinners, as he was." (Spurgeon)

        ii. Now is our time of *fiery trial* (1 Peter 4:12); the ungodly will have their fire later. The fire we endure now purifies us; the fire the ungodly will endure will punish them. Yet we always remember that there is never any punishment from God for us in our sufferings, only purification. For the Christian, the issue of *punishment* was settled once and for all at the cross, where Jesus endured all the punishment the Christian could ever face from God.

        iii. The same fire that consumes straw will purify gold. The fire is the same, but its *purpose* in application is different, and its *effect* is different upon the straw and the gold. Even so, Christians do suffer some of the same things the ungodly do, yet the *purpose* of God is different and the *effect* is different.

    b. **If it begins with us first, what will be the end of those who do not obey the gospel of God?** Peter's sobering application is clear. If this is what God's *children* experience, what will become of those who have made themselves His enemies? How can they ever hope to stand before the judgment and wrath of God?

        i. Christians can rejoice that the sufferings they face in this life are the worst they will ever face throughout all eternity. We have seen the worst; those who reject Jesus Christ have seen the *best* of life their eternal existence will ever see.

    c. **If the righteous one is scarcely saved**: Since this is true – that the salvation of the righteous does not come without difficulty – then it should make us pause if we ourselves or others seem to have an easy salvation.

i. It isn't that our salvation is difficult in the sense of earning it or finding a way to deserve it; it is all the free gift of Jesus Christ. Yet our salvation *is* hard in the sense that the claims of discipleship challenge us and demand that we cast away our idols and our sins. Real discipleship and genuine following after Jesus Christ is sometimes a hard thing, so we understand why Peter quoted the passage from Proverbs 11:31, "**the righteous one is scarcely saved.**"

d. **Those who suffer according to the will of God**: Peter again made a distinction between those **who suffer according to the will of God** and those who suffer otherwise. Not all suffering is the will of God.

e. **Commit their souls to Him**: The ancient Greek word translated "**commit**" is a technical one, used for leaving money on deposit with a trusted friend. Such a trust was regarded as one of the most sacred things in life, and the friend was bound by honor to return the money intact. It is the very word Jesus used when He said, "*Father, into Your hands I commit My spirit*" (Luke 23:46).

i. So when Christians **commit their souls to Him**, they leave their souls in a safe place. God is **a faithful Creator**, and we can give ourselves to Him as pliable clay in His hands.

f. **Faithful Creator**: Much of the agony we put ourselves through in times of trial and suffering has to do with our disregard of God's faithfulness or of His place as Creator. He *is* our sovereign **Creator**, with the right to do with us as He pleases. Yet He *is* **faithful**, and will only do what is ultimately best for us.

1 Peter 5 - For Shepherds and Sheep

A. Elders should be faithful shepherds.

1. (1) A call to elders.

The elders who are among you I exhort, I who am a fellow elder and a witness of the sufferings of Christ, and also a partaker of the glory that will be revealed:

a. **The elders who are among you I exhort**: Peter will give a word of exhortation to **the elders who are among** the Christians reading this letter. These elders had special responsibilities that Peter addressed.

i. The idea of the **elder** came into church life from Jewish culture (Exodus 3:16, 12:21, and 19:7). The word "**elder**" simply speaks of the maturity and wisdom that an older person should have, making them qualified for leadership. In its application, it is more about wisdom and maturity than a specific age.

ii. It was the practice of Paul and Barnabas to appoint elders in the churches they had founded (Acts 14:23). There was also the development of the office of pastor, who was essentially a teaching elder (1 Timothy 5:17) who appointed and guided elders and other leaders (1 Timothy 3:1-13, 2 Timothy 2:2, Titus 1:5-9).

b. **I who am a fellow elder**: Peter was qualified to speak because he is **a fellow elder**. Though Peter was clearly the prominent disciple among the twelve, he claimed no special privilege or position, such as being the pope of the early church. Instead, Peter saw himself only as one **fellow elder** among all the elders in the church.

i. "It will always be our wisdom, dear friends, to put ourselves as much as we can into the position of those whom we address. It is a pity for anyone ever to seem to preach down to people; it is always better to be as nearly as possible on the same level as they are." (Spurgeon)

c. **A witness of the sufferings of Christ, and also a partaker of the glory that will be revealed**: Peter was qualified to speak because he was a **witness** of Jesus' sufferings when he saw Jesus' torture and perhaps the crucifixion. He was also a **partaker** of Jesus' glory, probably referring to when he saw the transfiguration of Jesus.

i. "He was with Christ in the *garden*, he was with him when he was *apprehended*, and he was with him in the *high priest's hall*. Whether he followed him to the *cross* we know not." (Clarke)

ii. "The gospels do not state that Peter was personally present at the crucifixion; only John is specifically said to have been there. Peter (and other apostles) may well have been among 'all his acquaintances' who observed the event from afar (Luke 23:49)." (Hiebert)

iii. Considering that Peter may have – or likely did – witness the sufferings of Jesus on the cross, the remembrance of that would make his exhortation to fellow elders all the more powerful. It would be as if he said, "You are leaders of the people for whom Jesus Christ suffered and died, and I saw Him suffer."

iv. Yet we also consider that many saw Jesus suffer, and it did not affect them the way it affected Peter and others who saw with faith. "There were thousands who were eyewitnesses of our Lord's sufferings who, nevertheless, saw not the true meaning of them. They saw the Great Sufferer besmeared with his own blood; but into his wounds they never looked by faith. Thousands saw the Savior die, but they simply went their way back to Jerusalem, some of them beating on their breasts, but none of them believing in him, or really knowing the secret of that wondrous death." (Spurgeon)

2. (2-3) What leaders in the church must do.

Shepherd the flock of God which is among you, serving as overseers, not by compulsion but willingly, not for dishonest gain but eagerly; nor as being lords over those entrusted to you, but being examples to the flock;

a. **Shepherd the flock of God**: This was the first aspect of leadership. Peter seemed to remember Jesus' three-part commission to him in John 21:15-17. In that passage Jesus told Peter to show his love for Jesus by feeding and tending Jesus' sheep.

i. A spiritual **shepherd** does his job in two main ways. The first job is to *feed* the sheep. Jesus emphasized this to Peter in John 21:15-17. Another aspect of the job is to *tend* the sheep, which means protecting, guiding, nurturing, and caring for the sheep.

ii. The most important "tool" to **shepherd the flock of God** is a heart like the heart of Jesus, one that is willing to give one's life for the sheep, and who genuinely cares about and is interested in them (John 10:11-14).

b. **Serving as overseers**: For Peter the job of being a shepherd could also be understood as being an **overseer**. This word for leadership comes to the church from Greek culture, and it meant someone who watches over, a manager, or a supervisor (Acts 20:28, 1 Timothy 3:1-2, Titus 1:7).

c. **Not by compulsion but willingly**: Shepherds should not do their job by **compulsion**, as if they were being forced into a task that they really hated. Instead they should serve God and His people **willingly**, from a heart that loves God's people as a shepherd loves sheep and wants to serve them.

i. "None of God's soldiers are mercenaries or pressed men: they are all volunteers. We must have a shepherd's heart if we would do a shepherd's work." (Meyer)

d. **Not for dishonest gain but eagerly**: Spiritual shepherds should not do their job for **dishonest gain**. The gain is **dishonest** because it was their motive for serving as shepherds. Instead, they should serve **eagerly**, willing to serve apart from financial compensation.

i. "Could the office of a *bishop*, in those early days, and in the time of persecution, be a *lucrative* office? Does not the Spirit of God lead the apostle to speak these things rather for *posterity* than for that time?" (Clarke)

e. **Nor as being lords over those entrusted to you, but being examples to the flock**: Shepherds should not do their job as **lords**, because the sheep do not belong to them. The sheep are **entrusted** to them. Therefore shepherds are to serve by being **examples**, not dictators.

i. **Nor as being lords** shows that in the mind of Peter, shepherds had significant authority in the early church. If the office of shepherd was so powerless that a shepherd didn't rule and lead, then there was little potential for **being lords**. Yet because Peter gives this warning, it shows there was the potential for lording over.

ii. The sobering fact is that pastors *are* **examples to the flock**, whether they intend to be or not. It is interesting to see how a congregation takes on the personality of its pastor in both good ways and bad ways.

iii. **Those entrusted to you**: "That noun means 'a lot,' and then 'that which is assigned by lot,' a portion or a share of something. . . . God has assigned the various portions of His precious possession to their personal care." (Hiebert) The idea is that God has entrusted the responsibility of the spiritual care of certain individuals to particular shepherds.

3. (4) The reward for leaders in the church.

And when the Chief Shepherd appears, you will receive the crown of glory that does not fade away.

a. **When the Chief Shepherd appears**: Peter reminded shepherds in the church that they would answer one day to their **Chief Shepherd**, who will want to know what they did with *His* flock.

i. It is important for shepherds - pastors - to realize that they lead *Jesus'* sheep. *He* is the Shepherd, *He* is the Overseer (1 Peter 2:25). In this sense, the Christian shepherd doesn't work for the sheep, he works for the **Chief Shepherd**.

b. **You will receive a crown of glory**: Faithful shepherds are promised a **crown of glory**, but not like the crown of leaves given to ancient Olympic champions. This crown will **not fade away**.

i. Crowns are not only for shepherds, but also for everyone who was faithful to Jesus and who did what He called them to do (1 Corinthians 9:25, 2 Timothy 4:8, James 1:12).

B. Everyone should be humble and watchful.

1. (5-7) A promise for the humble.

Likewise you younger people, submit yourselves to *your* elders. Yes, all of *you* be submissive to one another, and be clothed with humility, for "God resists the proud, but gives grace to the humble." Therefore humble yourselves under the mighty hand of God, that He may exalt you in due time, casting all your care upon Him, for He cares for you.

a. **Likewise you younger people**: Peter began this word of humility to **you younger people**, in contrast to the elders he had just addressed. But he soon realized that it is of application to **all of you**. This word to **be submissive to one another and be clothed with humility** applies to everyone, but perhaps *especially* to the young.

b. **Clothed with humility**: **Humility** is demonstrated by submission. It is the ability to cheerfully put away our own agenda for God's, even if God's agenda is expressed through another person.

i. **Yes, all of you** means that this is for all, both elders and "youngers." "Strive all to serve each other; let the pastors strive to serve the people, and the people the pastors; and let there be no contention, but who shall do most to oblige and profit all the rest." (Clarke)

c. **Be clothed with humility**: The phrase "**be clothed**" translates a rare word that referred to a slave putting on an apron before serving, even as Jesus did before washing the disciple's feet (John 13:4).

i. Some marks of humility:

- The willingness to perform the lowest and littlest services for Jesus' sake.

- Consciousness of our own inability to do anything apart from God.

- The willingness to be ignored of men.

- Not so much self-hating or depreciation as self-forgetfulness, and being truly others-centered instead of self-centered.

d. **For "God resists the proud, but gives grace to the humble"**: Peter quoted Proverbs 3:34 to show that humility is essential to our relationship with God. If we want to live in God's **grace** (His unmerited favor) then we must lay aside our pride and be **humble** - not only to Him but also to one another.

i. **Resists**: "The verb vividly pictures God as one who places Himself in battle array against such individuals." (Hiebert)

ii. Grace and pride are eternal enemies. Pride demands that God bless me in light of what I think I deserve. Grace deals with me on the basis what is in God, not on the basis of anything in me.

iii. "Pride is one of the most detestable of sins; yet does it find lodgment in earnest souls, though we often speak of it by some lighter name. We call it - independence, self-reliance. We do not always discern it in the hurt feeling, which retires into itself, and nurses its sorrows in a sulk . . . We are proud of our humility, vain of our meekness; and, putting on the saintliest look, we wonder whether all around are not admiring us for our lowliness." (Meyer)

iv. "If you are willing to be nothing God will make something of you. The way to the top of the ladder is to begin at the lowest round. In fact in the church of God, the way up is to go down; but he that is ambitious to be at the top will find himself before long at the bottom." (Spurgeon)

e. **That He may exalt you in due time**: If God has us in a humble place at the present time, we must submit to God's plan. He knows the **due time** to exalt us, though we often think we know that time better than God does.

f. **Casting all your care upon Him**: True humility is shown by our ability to cast our **care upon** God. It is proud presumption to take things into our own worry and care about things that God has promised to take care of (Matthew 6:31-34).

i. If we would heed the command of 1 Peter 5:6 and truly humble ourselves under the mighty hand of God, we would have far fewer cares to cast upon Him as invited in 1 Peter 5:7. Worries about covetousness, ambition, popularity, all evaporate under the command to *humble yourselves under the mighty hand of God.*

ii. Spurgeon used the illustration of a man who came to move your furniture, but he carried a huge and heavy backpack of his own. He complains that he finds it difficult to do the job of moving your furniture; would you not suggest that he would find it easier if he laid his own burden aside so that he could carry yours? In the same way, we cannot do God's work when we are weighed down by our own burdens and worries. Cast them upon Him, and then take up the Lord's burden – which is light burden, and a yoke that fits us perfectly.

iii. There are many anxieties that we cannot cast upon God, and Peter's word here purifies us of these ungodly anxieties.

- "I am worried that I will never be rich."
- "I am burdened that others enjoy sinful pleasures and I do not."
- "I am worried that I am not famous or even popular."
- "I am burdened that I cannot get revenge on those who wronged me."

iv. "All cares of covetousness, anger, pride, ambition, and wilfulness must be cast to the winds; it would be criminal to dream of casting them upon God. Do not pray about them, except that God will redeem you from them. Let your desires be kept within a narrow circle, and your anxieties will be lessened at a stroke." (Spurgeon)

v. **Casting** is a rather energetic word. He didn't say, "Lay all your care upon Him," because we have to do it more energetically than that. The idea is, *"throw it away from you."* The pressures and the burdens of your life are so heavy and difficult that it takes great concentration of effort to put them on Jesus.

vi. This work of **casting** can be so difficult that we need to use two hands to do it: the hand of *prayer* and the hand of *faith.* "Prayer tells God what the care is, and asks God to help, while faith believes that God can and will do it. Prayer spreads the letter of trouble and grief before the Lord, and opens ail its budget, and then faith cries, 'I believe that God cares, and cares for me; I believe that he will bring me out of my distress, and make it promote his own glory.'" (Spurgeon)

g. **For He cares for you**: At their best moments the religions of ancient Greek culture could imagine a God who was good. Yet they never came to the place where they believed in a God who *cared*. The God of the Bible - the God who is really there - is a God who **cares for you**.

i. "It is the belief that God cares that marks off Christianity from all other religions, which under all varieties of form are occupied with the task of making God care, of awakening by sacrifice or prayer or act the slumbering interest of the Deity." (Masterman, cited in Hiebert)

ii. We often judge the parents by the children. When a child of God is full of worry and fear, doesn't the world have reason to believe that their Father in heaven doesn't care for them? Our worry and fear reflects poorly – and unfairly – upon God.

2. (8-9) Be watchful for the devil.

Be sober, be vigilant; because your adversary the devil walks about like a roaring lion, seeking whom he may devour. Resist him, steadfast in the faith, knowing that the same sufferings are experienced by your brotherhood in the world.

a. **Your adversary the devil walks about**: Peter exhorts us to remain clear-headed (**sober**) and watchful (**vigilant**), because Satan has not yet been bound and restrained for 1,000 years as Revelation 20:1-2 says he will be. At the present time, **the devil walks about**.

i. "He *walketh about*-he has access to you everywhere; he knows your feelings and your propensities, and informs himself of all your circumstances; only God can know more and do more than he, therefore your care must be cast upon God." (Clarke)

ii. The devil certainly **walks about**; he is a finite being and can only be in one place at one time, yet his effort, energy, and associates enable him to extend his influence all over the world and in every arena of life.

b. **Like a roaring lion**: For Christians, Satan is a **lion** who may roar but who has been de-fanged at the cross (Colossians 2:15). Yet the sound of his roar - his deceptive lies - are still potent and he has the power to **devour** souls and rob Christians of effectiveness.

i. Psalm 91:3 suggests that Satan may come against us like a *fowler*, one who captures birds. The fowler is always quiet and secretive, never wanting to reveal his presence. 2 Corinthians 11:14 tells us that Satan can come as *an angel of light*, appearing glorious, good, and attractive. Yet other times, Peter tells us, Satan comes against us **like a roaring lion**, loud and full of intimidation.

- He roars through persecution.
- He roars through strong temptation.
- He roars through blasphemies and accusations against God.

ii. We note Satan's goal: **seeking whom he may devour**. He isn't just looking to lick or nibble on his prey; he wants to **devour**. "He can never be content till he sees the believer utterly devoured. He would rend him in pieces, and break his bones and utterly destroy him if he could. Do not, therefore, indulge the thought, that the main purpose of Satan is to make you miserable. He is pleased with that, but that is not his ultimate end. Sometimes he may even make you happy, for he hath dainty poisons sweet to the taste which he administers to God's people. If he feels that our destruction can be more readily achieved by sweets than by bitters, he certainly would prefer that which would best effect his end." (Spurgeon)

c. **Resist him, steadfast in the faith**: The secret of spiritual warfare is simple, **steadfast** *resistance*. As we are **steadfast in the faith**, we **resist** the devil lies and threats and intimidation.

i. "Scripture urges believers to flee from various evils (1 Corinthians 6:18; 10:14; 1 Timothy 6:11; 2 Timothy 2:22), but nowhere are they advised to flee from the devil. That would be a futile effort." (Hiebert)

ii. **Resist** comes from two ancient Greek words: *stand* and *against*. Peter tells us to *stand against* the devil. Satan can be set running by the resistance of the lowliest believer who comes in the authority of what Jesus did on the cross.

iii. "Resist. Be more prayerful every time he is more active. He will soon give it up, if he finds that his attacks drive you to Christ. Often has Satan been nothing but a big black dog to drive Christ's sheep nearer to the Master." (Spurgeon)

d. **Knowing that the same sufferings are experienced by your brotherhood in the world**: We also take comfort in knowing that we are never alone in our spiritual warfare. Our brothers and sisters in Jesus have fought, and are fighting, the same battles.

i. "The outlook is on the whole conflict of the saints. It is seen as one. No soul is fighting alone. Each one is at once supporting, and supported by, all the rest." (Morgan)

3. (10-11) A prayer for their spiritual strengthening.

But may the God of all grace, who called us to His eternal glory by Christ Jesus, after you have suffered a while, perfect, establish, strengthen, and settle *you*. To Him *be* the glory and the dominion forever and ever. Amen.

a. **May the God of all grace . . . perfect, establish, strengthen, and settle you**: Knowing the suffering and danger Christians face, Peter can only conclude with *prayer*. He asks God to do His work of perfecting, establishing, strengthening, and settling.

i. These things are God's work in us and through us. Peter personally knew the futility of trying to face suffering and danger in one's own strength. His own failure taught him the need for constant reliance on God's work in our lives, so he prays for his dear Christian friends.

ii. **After you have suffered a while**: We almost want to ask Peter, "Why did you say that?" But the truth remains. We are only **called . . . to His eternal glory . . . after you have suffered a while**. We wish we were called to His eternal glory on the "no suffering" plan. But God uses suffering to **perfect, establish, strengthen, and settle** us.

iii. We are **called us to His eternal glory**; but what does this glory entail?

- It is the glory of purified character.
- It is the glory of perfected humanity.
- It is the glory of complete victory.
- It is the glory of being honored by a King.
- It is the glory of reflecting the glory of God.
- It is the glory of the immediate, constant presence of God.
- It is the glory of the enjoyment of God Himself.

b. **To Him be the glory and the dominion forever and ever**: The God who can do this great work in our lives is certainly worthy of our praise.

4. (12-14) Conclusion to the letter.

By Silvanus, our faithful brother as I consider him, I have written to you briefly, exhorting and testifying that this is the true grace of God in which you stand. She who is in Babylon, elect together with *you*, greets you; and *so does* Mark my son. Greet one another with a kiss of love. Peace to you all who are in Christ Jesus. Amen.

a. **By Silvanus . . . I have written to you**: This portion was probably written by Peter's own hand, after he (according to the custom of the day) had dictated the bulk of the letter to **Silvanus**. This man **Silvanus** was probably the same one known as *Silas* in many of Paul's letters.

b. **This is the true grace of God in which you stand**: Peter summed up his message as an exhortation to understand and recognize **the true grace of God in which you stand**. We must understand not only what God's grace is, but that grace is our place of present standing before Him.

c. **She who is in Babylon . . . greets you**: **She** probably refers to the church, which in the ancient Greek is in the feminine. Peter apparently wrote from **Babylon**. This may be the literal city of Babylon (which still existed in Peter's day), or it may be a symbolic way of referring to either Rome or

Jerusalem. These were two cities that in Peter's day were famous for their wickedness and spiritual rebellion, just like ancient **Babylon** was. In any regard, this was one church greeting another.

i. There was of course the literal city of Babylon on the Euphrates. There was also a place known as Babylon in Egypt, and it was a Roman military fortress near the present city of Cairo. Yet many think that Peter meant "Babylon" in a symbolic sense to represent the city of Rome. As a Biblical concept, "Babylon" as the city of this world stands in contrast to "Jerusalem" as the city of God. He may have meant Rome as Babylon as "the center of worldliness."

d. **So does Mark my son**: This verse connects **Mark** with Peter, apparently the same Mark of Acts 12:12, 12:25, and 15:37-39. When the style and perspective of the Gospel of Mark are taken into account, many believe that Peter was Mark's primary source of information for his gospel.

e. **Greet one another with a kiss of love**: Peter concludes with a command to greet and display God's love to one another, and by pronouncing a blessing of **peace**. These two things - **love** for each other and **peace** - are especially necessary for those who suffer and live in dangerous times.

i. "It should be noted that the apostles did not originate that form of greeting; the custom already prevailed. They sanctioned its use as a sincere expression of Christian love." (Hiebert)

2 Peter 1 - The Sure Christian Life

A. An encouragement to know God and what He has done for us.

1. (1) Introducing a letter from Peter, to believers.

Simon Peter, a bondservant and apostle of Jesus Christ, To those who have obtained like precious faith with us by the righteousness of our God and Savior Jesus Christ:

a. **Simon Peter**: The Apostle here called himself *Simon* Peter. Perhaps, since he wrote this letter later in life, he didn't want to forget where he came from and that sometimes he was still more like the old **Simon** than the new **Peter**.

i. We remember that **Simon** was his given name at birth; **Peter** was the special name given to him by Jesus, to call this man to "rock-like" thinking and behavior.

ii. Some have said that Peter didn't write this letter because the subject and style is somewhat different than 1 Peter. Yet the *purpose* of the two letters is quite different. 1 Peter was written to encourage Christians under the threat of violent persecution; 2 Peter was written to warn those same believers of the danger of false teachers and harmful influences.

iii. "Convinced that the **best antidote for heresy** is a **mature knowledge** of the truth, Peter exhorts his readers to have a proper appreciation for prophecy, to live holy and godly lives while awaiting Christ's coming and to grow in the grace and knowledge of the Lord." (Kirby)

b. **A bondservant and apostle of Jesus Christ**: The order of these titles is important. Peter considered himself *first* **a bondservant**, and *then* an **apostle**. His standing as a **bondservant** was more important to him than his status as an **apostle**.

c. **To those who have obtained like precious faith**: Peter wrote to those who had the same salvation he had experienced, which he called "a **like precious faith**." This faith was **obtained**, and not by the efforts of man but **by the righteousness of our God**.

i. "He tells us too, that faith is 'precious;' and is it not precious? For it deals with precious things, with precious promises, with precious blood, with a precious redemption, with all the preciousness of the person of our Lord and Savior Jesus Christ." (Spurgeon)

ii. **Like precious faith** probably speaks to the fact that the Jews and Gentiles enjoyed the same **faith**, and therefore the same benefits in Jesus. "God having given to *you* – believing *Gentiles*, the same faith and salvation which he had give to *us* – believing *Jews*." (Clarke)

d. **Our God and Savior Jesus Christ**: The grammar of the ancient Greek demonstrates that Peter said that **Jesus Christ** *is* **our God and Savior**. Peter clearly thought that Jesus was and is **our God and Savior**.

i. "The expression *God and our Saviour* is in a construction in the Greek text which demands that we translate, *our God and Saviour, Jesus Christ*, the expression thus showing that Jesus Christ is the Christian's God." (Wuest)

ii. "The grammar leaves little doubt that in these words Peter is calling Jesus Christ both God and Savior." (Blum)

2. (2-4) A greeting expanded into an understanding of the value of the knowledge of God.

Grace and peace be multiplied to you in the knowledge of God and of Jesus our Lord, as His divine power has given to us all things that *pertain* to life and godliness, through the knowledge of Him who called us by glory and virtue, by which have been given to us exceedingly great and precious promises, that through these you may be partakers of the divine nature, having escaped the corruption *that is* in the world through lust.

a. **Grace and peace be multiplied to you**: Peter indicated that **grace and peace** - those two most precious of gifts - are ours **in the knowledge of God and Jesus our Lord**. As we know God we gain these essentials foundations for salvation and living.

b. **His divine power has given to us all things that pertain to life and godliness**: However, not only grace and peace – but also **all things that pertain to life and godliness** are ours **through the knowledge of Him**. Knowing God is the key to **all things that pertain to life and godliness**.

i. These things come to us through **His divine power**. "Divine power! What stupendous issues are grasped in that term, divine power! It was this which digged the deep foundations of the earth and sea! Divine power, it is this which guides the marches of the stars of heaven! Divine power! it is this which holds up the pillars of the universe, and which one day shall shake them, and hurry all things back to their native nothingness." (Spurgeon)

ii. We are willing to try almost anything except **the knowledge of Him**. We will trust in the schemes and plans of men instead of **the knowledge of Him**. We will try knowing ourselves instead of **the knowledge of Him**. We need to come to the same place the Apostle Paul did, when he said *that I may know Him* (Philippians 3:10).

iii. According to Blum, the ancient Greek word **knowledge** doesn't refer to a casual acquaintance. It means an exact, complete, and thorough knowledge.

c. **Through the knowledge of Him**: We come to **knowledge of Him** as we learn of Him through His Word, through prayer, and through the community of God's people. It is true that we need God alone, but God does not meet us only in our solitude but also in the community of His people.

d. **Who called us**: This knowledge of God comes to those who are **called**. It is knowledge, but it is not mere intellectual understanding or intuition. It is the knowledge that comes by experience - the experience God's people have of God Himself.

e. **Who called us by glory and virtue**: It is Jesus' **glory and virtue** that motivated Him to call us, and it is His **glory and virtue** that draw us to Him.

f. **By which have been given to us exceedingly great and precious promises**: This explains the value of the **glory and virtue** of God that calls us. By these He gave us **exceedingly great and precious promises**. This means that the promises of God are based upon His **glory and virtue**, and therefore perfectly reliable because God can never compromise His **glory and virtue**.

i. Psalm 138:2 reminds us that God honors His word even above His name. We never have to doubt any promise of God. Instead we should *let God be true but every man a liar* (Romans 3:4).

ii. For these reasons, God's promises are both **exceedingly great** (in the sense of being large and imposing), and they are **precious**, in the sense of being valuable. "Many things are great which are not precious, such as great rocks, which are of little value; on the other hand, many things are precious which are not great-such as diamonds and other jewels, which cannot be very great if they be very precious. But here we have promises which are so great, that they are not less than infinite, and so precious, that they are not less than divine." (Spurgeon)

iii. "It was of considerable consequence to the comfort of the Gentiles that these promises were made to *them*, and that salvation was not exclusively of the Jews." (Clarke)

g. **That through these you may be partakers of the divine nature**: This explains the value of these **great and precious promises**. Through these

promises, we are **partakers of the divine nature**. Peter's idea is similar to Paul's idea of our glorious status as adopted sons and daughters of God (Galatians 4:5-7).

> i. This is a remarkably generous and loving of God. He could rescue us from hell without even inviting us to be **partakers of the divine nature**. It shows how deeply God loves us and wants to share His life – indeed, even **the divine nature** – with His people.

h. **Having escaped the corruption that is in the world through lust**: God is above and beyond the **corruption** of this world. It should also be that way with those who are the **partakers of the divine nature**. The **corruption that is in the world** expresses itself **through lust** - the ungodly desires of this world.

3. (5-7) How to live as a partaker of the nature.

But also for this very reason, giving all diligence, add to your faith virtue, to virtue knowledge, to knowledge self-control, to self-control perseverance, to perseverance godliness, to godliness brotherly kindness, and to brotherly kindness love.

a. **Giving all diligence**: We are *partakers of the divine nature*, but once we are made spiritual sons and daughters, growth in the Christian life doesn't just happen to us. We are supposed to give **all diligence** to our walk with the Lord.

b. **Add to your faith virtue**: We begin our life with God with **faith**, but faith progresses into **virtue, knowledge, self-control, perseverance, godliness, brotherly kindness**, and **love** - love being the capstone of all God's work in us.

> i. **Add to your faith**: Literally in the ancient Greek, "*Lead up hand in hand*; alluding, as most think, to the *chorus* in the Grecian dance, who danced with joined hands." (Clarke)

> ii. The scope of the list demonstrates that God wants us to have a well-rounded Christian life, complete in every fashion. We can't be content with an incomplete Christian life.

> iii. Of the word **self-control**, the Greek scholar Kenneth Wuest says the Greeks used this word **self-control** to describe someone who was not ruled by the desire for sex.

c. **Giving all diligence**: These beautiful qualities are not things that the Lord simply pours into us as we passively receive. Instead, we are called to give **all diligence** to these things, working in partnership with God to **add** them.

4. (8-9) How to use these qualities to measure our Christian walk.

For if these things are yours and abound, *you will be* **neither barren nor unfruitful in the knowledge of our Lord Jesus Christ. For he who lacks these things is shortsighted, even to blindness, and has forgotten that he was cleansed from his old sins.**

a. **If these things are yours and abound**: If we have these things, and **abound** in these things, it is evident to everyone that we are not **barren nor unfruitful** in our **knowledge** of Jesus.

i. The words **barren** and **unfruitful** characterize the lives of many Christians, who lack these qualities because they lack in their knowledge of God, that is, knowing Him relationally in an increasingly fuller and deeper sense.

ii. **Abound**: Some may feel good that these qualities are seen in us from time to time. But Peter says they should **abound** in us.

b. **He who lacks these things is shortsighted, even to blindness**: If we lack these things, it shows we have "eye trouble." We are **shortsighted**, unable to see God, only ourselves. This makes us virtually blind, showing we have **forgotten** that we were **cleansed from his old sins**.

i. "Such a man sees the things of time, and fails to discern those of eternity . . . he sees himself and his fellowmen, but not God. This nearsightedness is destructive of a true Christian experience, and therefore makes advance impossible." (Morgan)

ii. The *reason* for this condition is also stated; such a one **has forgotten that he was cleansed from his old sins**. "That is to say, he has failed to respond to all the enlargement of life and vision which came to him when he received the cleansing of his nature at the very beginning of his Christian life." (Morgan)

iii. Perhaps this one **has forgotten** how bad he was, and *how much he needed* this cleansing. Perhaps this one **has forgotten** the *great cost* of this purging of sin's dirty stain. Perhaps this one **has forgotten** how *great and complete* the cleansing is, making a once guilty sinner now as pure and as white as snow (Isaiah 1:18).

5. (10-11) Making our call and election sure.

Therefore, brethren, be even more diligent to make your call and election sure, for if you do these things you will never stumble; for so an entrance will be supplied to you abundantly into the everlasting kingdom of our Lord and Savior Jesus Christ.

a. **Be even more diligent to make your call and election sure**: This shows how we can be sure that God called us, and that we are His elect. It is by doing **these things** spoken of in 2 Peter 1:5-7 (*faith, virtue, knowledge, self-control, perseverance, godliness, brotherly kindness,* and *love*). As we see these things in our life, we know that our lives are becoming more like the nature of Jesus. It shows that we are being *conformed to the image of His Son* (Romans 8:29).

> i. It is possible for an unsaved person to do many moral and religious duties. But the "**these things**" Peter wrote of are matters of the heart, and should be evident in anyone *born again*. Simply said, if we are called, if we are elect, then we are born again - and if we are born again, it shows in the way that we live.

> ii. "It will be asked however, why is *calling* here put before *election* seeing election is eternal, and calling takes place in time? I reply, because calling is first to us. The first thing which you and I can know is our calling: we cannot tell whether we are elect until we feel that we are called. We must, first of all, prove our calling, and then our election is sure most certainly." (Spurgeon)

b. **For if you do these things you will never stumble**: In pursuing these things we keep from stumbling. Continual growth and progress in the Christian life is the sure way to keep from stumbling.

c. **Entrance will be supplied to you abundantly into the everlasting kingdom of our Lord and Savior Jesus Christ**: Peter here reminded his readers of the great reward of a **calling and election** made **sure**. They would enter heaven gloriously, not *as through fire* (1 Corinthians 3:15).

> i. "There are two ways of entering a port. A ship may come in, waterlogged and crazy, just keep afloat by continual working at the pumps; or it may enter with every sail set, her pennon floating at the masthead. The latter is what the apostle desires for himself and those who addresses. He desired that an entrance abundant should be ministered unto them." (Meyer)

> ii. F.B. Meyer also wrote that the idea of an "abundant entrance" was really a *choral entrance*. The idea was of a Roman conqueror coming into his city, welcomed by singers and musicians who would join him in a glorious, happy procession into the city.

> iii. "Will your entrance into heaven be like that? Will you enter it, save so as by fire, or to receive a reward? Will you come unrecognized and unknown, or be welcomed by scores and hundreds to whom you have been the means of blessing, and who will wait you?" (Meyer)

B. The need to be reminded.

1. (12) Peter explains why he writes about things they have heard before - the basics of Christian living.

For this reason I will not be negligent to remind you always of these things, though you know and are established in the present truth.

a. **For this reason**: Peter just wrote about the promise of *entrance* into *the everlasting kingdom* of God (2 Peter 1:11). Because coming to that kingdom is so important, it is helpful and necessary for Peter **to remind you always** of the basics of the Christian life.

b. **I will not be negligent to remind you always of these things, though you know**: Even though his readers did **know** the truth, in light of what was at stake - their eternal destiny - it was worth it to go over these ideas again and again.

i. A sports team going for the championship will practice the same fundamentals over and over again. They do this, even though they know the techniques, because they want the victory.

ii. For this reason, Christians should never get tired hearing the basics of the Christian life. We should rejoice every time Jesus Christ and His gospel and plan for our lives is preached.

c. **Established in the present truth**: **Established** is the same word translated *strengthen* in Luke 22:32, when Jesus told Peter "*when you have returned to Me, strengthen your brethren.*" Here, Peter fulfilled that command of Jesus. He would establish and strengthen us by reminding us of the basics of the Christian life.

2. (13-14) The urgency in Peter's heart.

Yes, I think it is right, as long as I am in this tent, to stir you up by reminding *you*, knowing that shortly I *must* put off my tent, just as our Lord Jesus Christ showed me.

a. **I think it is right**: Because of what is at stake, Peter knew it was **right** to remind people constantly, especially because he knew that the days of his earthly life were soon coming to an end.

b. **Shortly I must put off my tent**: Peter considered his body no more than a **tent**. A **tent** is a temporary place to live. Tents should be taken care of, but you wouldn't invest large resources into fixing up a tent. You save your real resources for a more permanent place to live. Our more permanent place to live is heaven, and we should invest more in heaven than in our **tent** – our physical body.

i. How did Peter know that *shortly* **I must put off my tent**? Perhaps it was because Peter was simply getting old. Perhaps it was because the flames of persecution were getting hotter around him. Church history tells us that Peter *did* die a martyr, **just as our Lord Jesus Christ showed** him (John 21:18-19).

ii. This shows that Peter believed that the prophetic words of Jesus were to be fulfilled literally. Jesus **showed** Peter that he would die a martyr, and he believed it - even if he might have *wished* it were only symbolic.

3. (15) Peter prepares for the future.

Moreover I will be careful to ensure that you always have a reminder of these things after my decease.

a. **I will be careful to ensure that you always have a reminder**: Peter put this reminder in a letter, so the people of God would have a constant reminder even after his departure.

b. **After my decease**: Peter seemed aware of the significance of the passing of the apostles and the need to preserve the authoritative teaching of the apostles and prophets. This, the written teaching of the apostles and their associates, is the foundation of the church (Ephesians 2:20) preserved by God for all generations.

C. The sureness of apostolic testimony.

1. (16-18) The evidence of the transfiguration.

For we did not follow cunningly devised fables when we made known to you the power and coming of our Lord Jesus Christ, but were eyewitnesses of His majesty. For He received from God the Father honor and glory when such a voice came to Him from the Excellent Glory: "This is My beloved Son, in whom I am well pleased." And we heard this voice which came from heaven when we were with Him on the holy mountain.

a. **We did not follow cunningly devised fables**: Peter solemnly declared that the testimony of the apostles - *testimony they endured torture and gave their lives for* - was not based on clever fables or even half truths, but on eyewitness testimony; that they **were eyewitnesses of His majesty**.

i. **Fables** translates the ancient Greek word *mythos*. Some people think the Gospel and the Biblical record are just ancient myths. They may admire their power as myths, but Peter rightly insisted that his message was no myth. It was history, seen by **eyewitnesses**.

ii. We can reliably reconstruct historical events from the testimony of **eyewitnesses**, who must be checked for truthfulness. The apostles and writers of the New Testament have been checked for centuries and have been found truthful.

b. **Eyewitnesses of His majesty**: When did Peter eyewitness the **majesty** of Jesus? There were many occasions, but one probably stuck out in his mind: the transfiguration of Jesus, recorded in Matthew 17:1-8, Mark 9:1-9, and Luke 9:28-36. We know this because Peter quoted here what God the Father said to Jesus at the Transfiguration: **"This is My beloved Son, in whom I am well pleased."**

> i. At the transfiguration, Jesus was *transformed* in glory before the apostles, not merely changed in outward appearance. The effect was extremely striking; Jesus became so bright in appearance that it was hard to look at Jesus. He shined *like the sun* (Matthew 17:2).

> ii. One may say that this shining glory was not a *new* miracle, but a pause in an ongoing miracle. The real miracle was that Jesus, most of the time, could *keep from* displaying His glory.

c. **This is My beloved Son, in whom I am well pleased**: At the transfiguration the Father spoke from heaven to declare His approval of and joy in God the Son. As Peter wrote this, we sense the words were still ringing in his ears because at the transfiguration he made the mistake of making Jesus equal with Moses and Elijah, who appeared along with Him.

> i. Those words from heaven were important because Jesus had just told His disciples that He would have to be crucified and His followers would also have to take up their cross to follow Him (Mark 8:31-38). His disciples needed this word of assurance to keep their confidence in Jesus and needed to hear that Jesus was still well pleasing to the Father, even though He said He would be crucified.

> ii. The words from heaven also clearly put Jesus above the Law and the Prophets. Jesus was not merely another or even a better lawgiver or prophet. Jesus was and is the **beloved Son**.

> iii. Essentially, the **voice** from heaven was a rebuke to Peter (Mark 9:7). Yet what was once a rebuke became a sweet memory.

> iv. Moses and Elijah appeared with Jesus because they represented those caught up to God (Jude 9 and 2 Kings 2:11). They represented the Law (Moses) and the Prophets (Elijah). Moses and Elijah also are connected with prophecy, having a strong connection to the witnesses of Revelation 11:3-13.

d. **And we heard this voice which came from heaven**: It was awesome for Peter and the disciples to see the transfigured, glorified Jesus. It was awesome for them to hear **this voice . . . from heaven**. Yet the experience itself did not transform their lives. Only being born again by the Spirit of God did that, giving them boldness beyond measure. The transfiguration was awesome, but it was a passing experience until they were born again.

2. (19) The evidence of fulfilled prophecy.

And so we have the prophetic word confirmed, which you do well to heed as a light that shines in a dark place, until the day dawns and the morning star rises in your hearts;

a. **And so we have the prophetic word confirmed**: Peter's experience at the transfiguration was amazing. But the testimony of God's word about Jesus was even more sure than Peter's personal experience. The fulfillment of **the prophetic word confirmed** is a certain, reliable testimony of the truth of the Scriptures.

i. "Taken according to the common translation, it seems to say that *prophecy* is a surer evidence of Divine revelation than *miracles*; and so it has been understood." (Clarke)

b. **Which you do well to heed**: When we consider the prophetic testimony to Jesus, we **do well to heed** it. There are at least 332 distinct Old Testament predictions regarding the Messiah that Jesus fulfilled perfectly. The combination of this evidence together, from a simple statistical perspective, is absolutely overwhelming.

i. Professor Peter Stoner has calculated that the probability of any one man fulfilling eight of these prophesies is one in 100,000,000,000,000,000 (10 to the 17th power). That number of silver dollars would cover the state of Texas two feet deep. Stoner says that if you consider 48 of the prophecies, the odds become one in 10 to the 157th power.

c. **As a light that shines in a dark place**: No wonder Peter could say that the prophetic word is **confirmed**, and that it is as a **light that shines in a dark place**, something we should cling to **until the day dawns** and Jesus returns.

3. (20-21) Principles for prophetic assurance.

Knowing this first, that no prophecy of Scripture is of any private interpretation, for prophecy never came by the will of man, but holy men of God spoke *as they were* moved by the Holy Spirit.

a. **No prophecy of Scripture is of any private interpretation**: Even in Peter's day enemies of Jesus twisted Old Testament prophecies, giving them personal and bizarre meanings attempting to exclude Jesus from their fulfillment. But Peter says that prophecy is not **of any private interpretation**; its meaning is evident and can be confirmed by others.

i. Though Peter here spoke of **prophecy of Scripture**, the same principle is true for the gift of prophecy today. There must be sober *confirmation* of any prophetic word, and that not through another prophetic word but through the Scriptures. In the gift of prophecy, God never speaks to *only* one person, and always provides confirmation.

b. **Prophecy never came by the will of man**: It is wrong and invalid to twist prophecy to our own personal meaning, because prophecy does not come from man but from God. It does come through **holy men of God** - but only as they are **moved by the Holy Spirit**.

i. "Far from *inventing* the subject of their own predictions, the ancient prophets did not even *know* the meaning of what they themselves wrote. They were *carried beyond themselves* by the influence of the *Divine Spirit*, and after ages were alone to discover the object of the prophecy; and the fulfillment was to be the absolute proof that the prediction was of God and that it was of no *private invention*." (Clarke)

c. **As they were moved by the Holy Spirit**: According to Green, the ancient Greek word translated "**moved**" has the sense of *carried along*, as a ship being carried along by the wind or the current (the same word is used of a ship in Acts 27:15, 17). It is as if the writers of Scripture "raised their sails" in cooperation with God and the Holy Spirit carried them along in the direction He wished.

2 Peter 2 - The Rise and Fall of False Teachers

A. Facts about false teachers.

1. (1) The presence and work of false teachers.

But there were also false prophets among the people, even as there will be false teachers among you, who will secretly bring in destructive heresies, even denying the Lord who bought them, *and* **bring on themselves swift destruction.**

a. **But there were also false prophets**: Even as there were *holy men of God who spoke as they were moved by the Holy Spirit* (2 Peter 1:21), so also there were **false prophets** and **false teachers** then and today. Peter stated this as a fact and not as a possibility; and he said they were **among you**, not only on the outside of the church.

i. "There were not only holy men of God among the Jews, who prophesied by divine inspiration, but there were also false prophets, whose prophecies were from their own imagination, and perverted many." (Clarke)

b. **Who will secretly bring in destructive heresies**: False teachers work **secretly**. It isn't that their teaching is secret, but the deceptive nature of their teaching is hidden. No false teacher ever announces himself as a false teacher.

c. **Destructive heresies**: False teachers bring in **destructive heresies** that destroy by telling lies about Jesus Christ and His work for us and in us. By these **heresies** people are hurt and destroyed. Heresy isn't harmless.

d. **Even denying the Lord who bought them**: False teachers deny the **Lord who bought them**. In this Peter says that at the very least, they *appear* to be saved. Otherwise Peter would never say that the Lord **bought them**. At the same time, they are false, destructive teachers.

i. Even a person who has what appears to be a godly walk and relationship with Jesus Christ can still bring in destructive heresies. Often times good men who teach lies do the worst damage. Their lies are accepted far more easily because of the good character of these men.

e. **Bring on themselves swift destruction**: False teachers are promised **swift destruction**, even though they aren't judged fast enough in the opinion of many.

2. (2) The popularity of false teachers.

And many will follow their destructive ways, because of whom the way of truth will be blasphemed.

a. **Many will follow their destructive ways**: This reminds us that false teachers may be popular. Just because something succeeds in attracting a crowd of followers, it doesn't mean that it is of God. We know that God's work will always bear fruit, but the devil's work can also increase.

i. The most distressing aspect of the work of false teachers is not that they are *among you* (2 Peter 2:1). False teachers always have been and always will be among Christians. The most distressing fact is that so many Christians **will follow their destructive ways**.

b. **Because of whom the way of truth will be blasphemed**: When false teachers are at work and when crowds are following them, the **way of truth** is **blasphemed**. God's holy name and honor are disgraced.

3. (3) The strategy and destiny of false teachers.

By covetousness they will exploit you with deceptive words; for a long time their judgment has not been idle, and their destruction does not slumber.

a. **By covetousness**: False teachers use **covetousness** - both their own and in their followers. Many false teachers, both today and in previous times, present a gospel that has self-gratification at its core. All this is presented **with deceptive words** because false teaching never announces itself.

b. **Their judgment has not been idle, and their destruction does not slumber**: Peter assured us that false teachers *will be* judged. Even though it seems they prosper, their judgment is not **idle**. God's wrath pours out on them even in allowing them to continue, thus heaping up more and more condemnation and hardness of heart in themselves.

B. God knows how to take care of both the righteous and the ungodly.

1. (4-6) The ungodly will be judged.

For if God did not spare the angels who sinned, but cast *them* down to hell and delivered *them* into chains of darkness, to be reserved for judgment; and did not spare the ancient world, but saved Noah, *one of* eight *people*, a preacher of righteousness, bringing in the flood on the world of the ungodly; and turning the cities of Sodom and Gomorrah

into ashes, condemned *them* **to destruction, making** *them* **an example to those who afterward would live ungodly;**

a. **If God did not spare the angels who sinned**: God judged these wicked angels, setting them in **chains of darkness**. Apparently some fallen angels are in bondage while others are unbound and active in the earth as demons.

i. The sin of angels can be thought of in two main ways: in the original rebellion of some angels against God, and in the sin of the "sons of God" described in Genesis 6:1-2.

ii. It is clear that at some time, angelic beings had a period of choosing and testing when their future destiny would be determined. "How long that probation was to last to them, and what was the particular *test* of their fidelity, we know not; nor indeed do we know what was their *sin*; nor *when* nor *how* they fell. Jude says *they kept not their first estate, but left their own habitation*; which seems to indicate that they got *discontented* with their lot, and aspired to higher honours, or perhaps to celestial domination." (Clarke)

iii. It may be that the sin of Satan and his angels (Revelation 12:4, 12:7) was occasioned by the plan of God for mankind.

- Man is made in the image of God (Genesis 1:26) and angels are not. Satan and his angels resented this plan to create a being that would be more closely connected to God than they were.

- Though mankind is beneath the angels in dignity (Hebrews 2:6-7a, 2 Peter 2:11), it is the job of angels to serve mankind (Hebrews 1:14, 2:7-8, Psalm 91:11-12). Satan and his angels resented a plan that would command them to serve lesser beings.

- Redeemed mankind will be lifted in honor and status above all angelic beings (1 Corinthians 6:3; 1 John 3:2). Satan and his angels resented a plan that would glorify these lower beings to places above them.

iv. "It sprang from the admiration of their own gifts, it was confirmed by pride and ambition, it was perfected by envy, stirred by the decree of exalting man's nature above angels in and by Christ." (Trapp)

v. At the same time, we cannot conclusively say we know *why* the angels sinned because the Scriptures do not give us more than hints.

b. **Cast them down to hell and delivered them into chains of darkness**: By not keeping their proper place, they are now kept in **chains of darkness**. Their sinful pursuit of freedom put them in bondage.

i. Those who insist on freedom to do whatever they want are like these angels: so "free" that they are bound with **chains of darkness** (a powerful poetic description of their miserable bondage). True freedom comes from obedience.

ii. **Cast them down to hell**: The ancient Greek word translated **hell** is literally *Tartarus*. In Greek mythology, Tartarus was the lowest hell, a place of punishment for rebellious gods. Peter borrowed this word to speak of the place of punishment for **the angels who sinned**.

iii. Angels have a high office and a high service of God; yet it was still possible for them to fall. We should take warning from this. As well, we can understand that in some ways we can sin worse than these angels did. "I answer that the devil never yet rejected free grace and dying love; the devil never yet struggled against the Holy Spirit in his own conscience; the devil never yet refused the mercy of God. These supreme pinnacles of wickedness are only reached by you who are hearers of the gospel, and yet cast its precious message behind your backs." (Spurgeon)

c. **And did not spare the ancient world**: God judged **the ancient world**, the world before Noah's Flood, because *the LORD saw that the wickedness of man was great in the earth, and that every intent of the thoughts of his heart was only evil continually* (Genesis 6:5).

d. **And turning the cities of Sodom and Gomorrah into ashes, condemned them to destruction**: God judged the cities of Sodom and Gomorrah, making them an example of His judgment, *because the outcry against Sodom and Gomorrah is great, and because their sin is very grave* (Genesis 18:20).

e. **Making them an example to those who afterward would live ungodly**: These three examples of judgment show us the important principle that Peter wants to highlight.

- God judged **the angels who sinned**, so *no one is too high to be judged*.
- God judged **the ancient world** before the flood, so *God doesn't grade on a curve*, only comparing man among other men.
- God judged **Sodom and Gomorrah**, so *even the prosperous can be judged*.

i. Therefore the **ungodly** have no reason to think they can escape God's judgment. Their coming judgment is certain. As Jesus said in Luke 10:10-12, for those who reject the truth *"it will be more tolerable in that Day for Sodom."*

2. (7-9) The righteous will be delivered.

And delivered righteous Lot, *who was* **oppressed by the filthy conduct of the wicked (for that righteous man, dwelling among them, tormented** *his* **righteous soul from day to day by seeing and hearing** *their* **lawless deeds);** *then* **the Lord knows how to deliver the godly out of temptations and to reserve the unjust under punishment for the day of judgment,**

a. **And delivered righteous Lot**: Peter already told us how the Lord delivered Noah (2 Peter 2:5). Now, he shows us that the Lord **delivered righteous Lot**.

i. "The preservation and deliverance of Lot gave the apostle occasion to remark, that God knew as well to *save* as to *destroy*; and that his *goodness* led him as forcibly to save righteous Lot, as his *justice* did to destroy the rebellious in the instances already adduced." (Clarke)

b. **And delivered righteous Lot**: Lot was **righteous** in God's eyes, though perhaps it was hard for others to see his righteousness. Yet the wickedness of Sodom and Gomorrah **tormented his righteous soul from day to day**.

i. Lot's **soul** was **tormented**, but he failed to follow through with godly actions and separate himself and his family from the ungodliness of Sodom and Gomorrah. The Lord **delivered** Lot because of his **righteous** soul; yet Lot lost everything else because of his too-close association with those wicked cities.

c. **Then the Lord knows how to deliver the godly out of temptations**: Even as the Lord delivered Lot, He knows how to deliver us from the **temptations** we face, and He knows how to **reserve the unjust** for the day of judgment. We can trust in God's deliverance of the godly because it is just as certain as His judgment of the ungodly.

i. **The Lord knows how**: We can take great confidence in this. Many times *we* do not know how, but **the Lord knows how**. This is a good principle for both life and doctrine. "For instance, sometimes we meet with perplexing doctrines; perhaps we endeavor to effect reconciliation between the predestination of God and the freedom of human action. It is better not to wade too far into those deep waters, lest we lose ourselves in an abyss. 'The Lord knoweth.'" (Spurgeon)

ii. The **unjust** have reservation made for them: they are reserved **for the day of judgment**. But believers have no such reservation. God will deliver us from the very day of judgment, from the very time of wrath that He pours out on the earth (Revelation 3:10).

iii. "According to the Revised Version, and I think that translation is correct, the punishment has begun already. The Lord knows how to go on even now punishing the ungodly." (Spurgeon)

iv. "Peter (if any man) might well say, 'The Lord knoweth how to deliver his;' for he had been strangely delivered, Acts 12." (Trapp) In Acts 12, God wonderfully delivered Peter from prison and He painfully delivered Herod to judgment. God knows how to do both.

C. A description of the ungodly among them.

1. (10-11) They are fleshly and proud.

And especially those who walk according to the flesh in the lust of uncleanness and despise authority. *They are* presumptuous, self-willed. They are not afraid to speak evil of dignitaries, whereas angels, who are greater in power and might, do not bring a reviling accusation against them before the Lord.

a. **And especially those who walk according to the flesh**: These ungodly ones are *especially* reserved for judgment. They live according to the flesh, not the spirit, and are marked by **uncleanness**.

b. **They are presumptuous, self-willed**: These ungodly ones are proud, despising authority. In their presumption they will even speak ill of spiritual powers (Satan and his demons) that the angels themselves do not speak evil of, but the angels rebuke them in the name of the Lord instead.

i. Much of what goes on under the name of spiritual warfare shows this kind of pride and presumption. While we recognize our authority in Jesus, we see that it is only in Jesus that we have it - and we leave the **reviling accusations** to Him alone.

c. **Whereas angels, who are greater in power and might, do not bring a reviling accusation**: Here Peter contrasted the behavior of **those who walk according to the flesh** with **angels**, that is, faithful angels. The faithful angels did not slander or exaggerate in what they said or how they represented the sins of others; these who walked according to the flesh did.

2. (12-13a) Their spiritual doom is sealed.

But these, like natural brute beasts made to be caught and destroyed, speak evil of the things they do not understand, and will utterly perish in their own corruption, *and* will receive the wages of unrighteousness, *as* those who count it pleasure to carouse in the daytime.

a. **Like natural brute beasts**: Since they function in the flesh, not the spirit, they are like animals. They are fit only for destruction (**made to be caught and destroyed**) and they are ignorant.

b. **And will receive the wages of unrighteousness**: The ungodly will be "paid" for their evil - and their fleshly lives will be paid the **wages of unrighteousness**.

i. "What these evil men, who were troubling Peter's people, were doing, was to say that they loved and served Christ, while the things they taught and did were a complete denial of him." (Barclay)

3. (13b-17) A list of the sins of the false teachers.

They are **spots and blemishes, carousing in their own deceptions while they feast with you, having eyes full of adultery and that cannot cease from sin, enticing unstable souls.** *They have* **a heart trained in covetous practices,** *and are* **accursed children. They have forsaken the right way and gone astray, following the way of Balaam the** *son* **of Beor, who loved the wages of unrighteousness; but he was rebuked for his iniquity: a dumb donkey speaking with a man's voice restrained the madness of the prophet. These are wells without water, clouds carried by a tempest, for whom is reserved the blackness of darkness forever.**

a. **Carousing in their own deceptions**: These ungodly false teachers are a dangerous and corrupting presence in the body of Christ, not only deceiving others but deceiving themselves also.

i. "The word here rendered riot [**carousing**], comes of a root that signifies to break, for there is nothing that doth so break and emasculate the minds of men as rioting and reveling; luxury draws out a man's spirits, and dissolves him." (Trapp)

b. **Having eyes full of adultery**: Their heart is set on the flesh, and their **eyes** on **adultery**, both spiritual and sexual. They prey on the unstable to join them in their ways (**enticing unstable souls**).

i. Literally, Peter wrote that *their eyes are full of an adulterous woman.* "They lust after every girl they see; they view every female as a potential adulteress." (Green)

c. **They have a heart trained in covetous practices**: They are equipped, but not for ministry, only for selfish gain - they are truly **accursed**. We all train our hearts in something, either training them in covetousness and lust, or in godliness.

i. "The metaphor is taken from the *agonistae* in the Grecian games, who exercised themselves in those feats, such as *wrestling, boxing, running, etc.*, in which they proposed to contend in the public games. These persons had their hearts schooled in nefarious practices; they had *exercised themselves* until they were perfectly *expert* in all the arts of seduction, overreaching, and every kind of fraud." (Clarke)

d. **Following the way of Balaam**: They are like Balaam, who was guilty of the greatest of sins – leading others into sin, and that for the sake of his own gain. Balaam had to be restrained by a **dumb donkey** because he would not listen to God.

e. **These are wells without water**: These ungodly false teachers are empty – as useless as **wells without water** – and like clouds that bring only darkness, and no nourishing rain.

4. (18-19) The allure of the false teachers.

For when they speak great swelling *words* of emptiness, they allure through the lusts of the flesh, through lewdness, the ones who have actually escaped from those who live in error. While they promise them liberty, they themselves are slaves of corruption; for by whom a person is overcome, by him also he is brought into bondage.

a. **They speak great swelling words of emptiness**: The message of the ungodly false teachers is empty of real spiritual content, though it is swollen big with words. Their allure is to the **lusts of the flesh** in their audience, just as the crowds who wanted bread from Jesus, but didn't want Jesus Himself (John 6:25-27, 6:47-66).

b. **While they promise them liberty, they themselves are slaves**: They promise freedom, but freedom can never be found in the flesh, only in God's Spirit. Freedom isn't found in what Jesus can *give* us, but only in Jesus Himself. When we seek freedom in the wrong way, we become **slaves of corruption** (decay and death).

c. **By him also he is brought into bondage**: In being overcome by the flesh and the false teachers, these unfortunates became slaves to both.

5. (20-22) The danger of falling away and following after false teachers

For if, after they have escaped the pollutions of the world through the knowledge of the Lord and Savior Jesus Christ, they are again entangled in them and overcome, the latter end is worse for them than the beginning. For it would have been better for them not to have known the way of righteousness, than having known *it*, to turn from the holy commandment delivered to them. But it has happened to them according to the true proverb: "A dog returns to his own vomit," and, "a sow, having washed, to her wallowing in the mire."

a. **The latter end is worse for them than the beginning**: It is better for a person to have never known a thing about Jesus than to hear some truth, hold to it for a seaon, and then later reject it. Greater revelation has a greater accountability.

i. Their **end is worse . . . than the beginning** because they have returned to **the pollutions of the world**. "These [**pollutions**] are called *miasmata*, things that *infect*, *pollute*, and *defile*. . . . St. Augustine has improved on this image: 'The whole world,' says he, 'is one great diseased man, lying extended from east to west, and from north to south; and to heal this great sick man, the almighty Physician descended from heaven.'" (Clarke)

b. **It would have been better for them not to have known the way of righteousness**: Peter described a picture that certainly has the *appearance* of people losing their salvation.

- He speaks of those who **have escaped the pollutions of the world**.

- He speaks of those who did this **through the knowledge of the Lord and Savior Jesus Christ**.

- He speaks of those who at one time had **known the way of righteousness**.

i. Christians warmly debate the issue of whether or not it is possible for a true Christian to ever lose their status as a true Christian and fall away to damnation. Perhaps the best way of understanding the issue is to say that it is certainly true that those who *appear* saved – those who fit the description of Peter here – can end up in a place where **it would have been better for them not to have known the way of righteousness**.

ii. Regarding these, those with a Reformed perspective will say that they were actually *never* saved; those with an Arminian perspective will say that they were actually saved and *lost their salvation*. To bitterly divide along the lines of this debate – which focuses on things that are unknowable to outside observation – seems to fall into the category of being *obsessed with disputes and arguments over words*, as in 1 Timothy 6:4.

c. **A dog returns to his own vomit**: The nature as **dogs** is displayed by the way he returns to the **vomit** of the flesh and the world. He is like the *brute beasts* described in 2 Peter 2:12, more animal than godly because he lives for the flesh.

i. "The dog which has got rid of the corruption inside it through vomiting it up cannot leave well enough alone; it goes sniffing around the vomit again." (Green)

2 Peter 3 - Living Like a "Last Days Christian"

A. The certainty of the last days and God's promise.

1. (1-2) Another reference to the importance of being reminded

Beloved, I now write to you this second epistle (in *both of* which I stir up your pure minds by way of reminder), that you may be mindful of the words which were spoken before by the holy prophets, and of the commandment of us, the apostles of the Lord and Savior,

a. **I now write to you this second epistle**: Peter already wrote about the importance of being reminded (2 Peter 1:12-13). But here he wanted to emphasize what should be known in light of the coming of Jesus and the prophecies surrounding His coming.

i. "The purest minds need stirring up at times. It would be a great pity to stir up impure minds. That would only be to do mischief; but pure minds may be stirred as much as you please, and the more the better." (Spurgeon)

b. **That you may be mindful of the words which were spoken before**: Peter knew the importance of *reminding* his readers of the Scriptural message, both received from the Old Testament (**spoken before**) and contemporary to his own day (**and of the commandment of us**).

i. Peter clearly believed that the **words** of Scripture were important; the **words** themselves, and not merely the *meaning* behind the words.

ii. "Peter believed in the inspiration of the very 'words' of Scripture; he was not one of those precious 'advanced thinkers' who would, if they could, tear the very soul out of the Book, and leave us nothing at all; but he wrote, 'That ye may be mindful of the words' — the very words — 'which were spoken before by the holy prophets.' 'Oh!' says one, 'but words do not signify; it is the inward sense that is really important.' Exactly so; that is just what the fool said about egg-shells. He said that they did not signify; it was only the inward life-germ of the chick within that was important; so he broke all the shells, and thereby destroyed the life. . . . If the words could be taken from us, the sense itself would be gone." (Spurgeon)

c. **By the holy prophets, and of the commandment of us, the apostles of the Lord and Savior**: By placing the messengers of the new covenant on the same level as the messengers of the old covenant, Peter understood the authority of the New Testament, even as it was being formed.

> i. Peter understood that Jesus gave His **apostles** the inspired authority to bring forth God's message to the new covenant community. He understood this from passages such as Matthew 16:19, where Jesus gave the apostles authority to *bind* and *loose*, much as the authoritative rabbis of their day.

> ii. "*Your apostles* does not merely mean 'your missionaries', the folk who evangelized you. When the New Testament writers mean merely 'church emissary' by *apostolos*, they say so, or the context makes it plain (Philippians 2:25). Peter is referring here to the 'apostles of Jesus Christ'. It is they and they alone who are put on a level with the Old Testament prophets." (Green)

> iii. Significantly, Peter saw this authority invested in **the apostles**, not in him alone. He would think it strange for supposed papal authority to be credited to him.

2. (3-4) The message of scoffers.

Knowing this first: that scoffers will come in the last days, walking according to their own lusts, and saying, "Where is the promise of His coming? For since the fathers fell asleep, all things continue as *they were* from the beginning of creation."

a. **Knowing this first**: Christians should not be surprised to find that there are those who scoff at the idea of Jesus coming again. Peter told us that the **scoffers will come**. This is the **first** thing to know.

> i. "Every time a blasphemer opens his mouth to deny the truth of revelation, he will help to confirm us in our conviction of the very truth which he denies. The Holy Ghost told us, by the pen of Peter, that it would be so; and now we see how truly he wrote." (Spurgeon)

b. **Will come in the last days**: In a sense, the **last days** began when Jesus ascended into heaven. Since that time, we haven't rushed towards the precipice of the consummation of all things; but we have run along side that edge - ready to go anytime at God's good pleasure.

> i. "With the advent of Jesus the last chapter of human history had opened, though it was not yet completed." (Green)

c. **Walking according to their own lusts**: These words remind us that scoffers do not only have an intellectual problem with God and His word. They also have a clear *moral* problem, wanting to reject the Lordship of Jesus Christ over their lives.

d. **Where is the promise of His coming?** This is the message of scoffers. In the thinking of these scoffers, Christians have talked about Jesus coming for two thousand years and He still hasn't come back yet.

e. **All things continue as they were from the beginning of creation**: The **scoffers** base their message on the idea that things have always been the way they are right now, and that God has not and will not do anything new in His plan for creation.

i. "The argument of the false teachers is essentially a naturalistic one – a kind of uniformitarianism that rules out divine intervention in history." (Blum)

3. (5-7) The error of scoffers.

For this they willfully forget: that by the word of God the heavens were of old, and the earth standing out of water and in the water, by which the world *that* then existed perished, being flooded with water. But the heavens and the earth *which* are now preserved by the same word, are reserved for fire until the day of judgment and perdition of ungodly men.

a. **For this they willfully forget**: The scoffers presume upon the mercy and longsuffering of God, insisting that because they have never seen a wide-spread judgment of God, that there will never be one. But **they willfully forget** God's creation and the judgment God poured out on the earth in the days of Noah.

i. A literal belief in Creation, in Adam and Eve, and in Noah's Flood are essential for a true understanding of God's working both then and now. To deny these things undermines the very foundations of our faith. Sadly, today it is many Christians who **willfully forget** these things, thereby putting themselves in the place of scoffers.

b. **That by the word of God the heavens were of old**: The Bible clearly teaches that the active agent in creation was God's **word**. He spoke and creation came into being.

c. **The world that then existed perished, being flooded with water**: Peter's point is that things on this earth have not always continued the way they are now. The earth was different when God first created it and then it was different again after the flood. Therefore no one should scoff at God's promise that He will make it different once again, judging it not with water but with fire. The same **word of God** that created all matter and judged the world in the flood will one day bring a judgment of fire upon the earth.

i. "The lesson taught by the flood was this is a moral universe, that sin will not for ever go unpunished; and Jesus himself used the flood to point to this moral (Matthew 24:37-39). But these men chose to neglect it." (Green)

4. (8-10) Truths that scoffers deny but God's people cling to.

But, beloved, do not forget this one thing, that with the Lord one day *is* **as a thousand years, and a thousand years as one day. The Lord is not slack concerning** *His* **promise, as some count slackness, but is longsuffering toward us, not willing that any should perish but that all should come to repentance. But the day of the Lord will come as a thief in the night, in which the heavens will pass away with a great noise, and the elements will melt with fervent heat; both the earth and the works that are in it will be burned up.**

a. **That with the Lord one day is as a thousand years, and a thousand years as one day**: What seems like forever for us is but a short time for God, just as an hour may seem to be an eternity for a child but a moment for an adult.

i. Peter quoted this idea from Psalm 90:4: *For a thousand years in Your sight are like yesterday when it is past, and like a watch in the night.* "All time is as nothing before him, because in the *presence* as in the *nature* of God all is *eternity*; therefore nothing is *long*, nothing *short*, before him; no *lapse* of ages impairs his purposes." (Clarke)

ii. "All things are equally near and present to his view; the distance of a thousand years before the occurrence of an event, is no more to him than would be the interval of a day. With God, indeed, there is neither past, present, nor future. He takes for his name the 'I AM.' . . . He is the I AM; I AM in the present; I AM in the past and I AM in the future. Just as we say of God that he is everywhere, so we may say of him that he is always; he is everywhere in space; he is everywhere in time." (Spurgeon)

iii. Peter did not give some prophetic formula, saying that a prophetic day somehow equals a thousand years. He instead communicated a general principle regarding how we see time and how God sees time. When people use this verse as a rigid prophetic key it opens the door for great error.

iv. "God sees time with a *perspective* we lack; even the delay of a thousand years may well seem like a day against the back-cloth of eternity. Furthermore, God sees time with an *intensity* we lack; one day with the Lord is like a thousand years." (Green)

b. **The Lord is not slack concerning His promise**: The truth is that God *will* keep His promise, and without delay according to His timing. Any perceived delay from our perspective is due to the **longsuffering** of God, who allows man as much time as possible to repent.

i. Many of those who are Christians today are happy that Jesus didn't return ten years, or five years, or two years, or one year, or even two months ago. There is a compassionate purpose in God's timing.

c. **Not willing that any should perish but that all should come to repentance**: Peter here revealed some of God's glorious heart. The reason why Jesus' return isn't sooner is so that **all should come to repentance**, because God is **not willing that any should perish**.

i. We understand that God is **not willing that any should perish** not in the sense of a divine decree, as if God has *declared* that no sinners will perish. Rather, Peter's statement reflects God's heart of love for the world (John 3:16), and His compassionate sorrow even in the righteous judgment of the wicked.

ii. It is the same thought as expressed in Ezekiel 33:11: *As I live, says the Lord GOD, I have no pleasure in the death of the wicked, but that the wicked turn from his way and live.*

iii. "So wonderful is his love towards mankind, that he would have them all to be saved, and is of his own self prepared to bestow salvation on the lost." (Calvin)

iv. "As God is *not willing that any should perish*, and as he is *willing that all should come to repentance*, consequently he has never devised nor decreed the damnation of any man, nor has he rendered it impossible for any soul to be saved." (Clarke)

d. **But the day of the Lord will come as a thief in the night**: Though the Lord's longsuffering love to the lost makes it seem that perhaps He delays His coming, the truth is that He will indeed come. And when Jesus does return, He will come at a time that will surprise many (**as a thief in the night**). The ultimate result of His coming will be a total transformation of this present world (**in which the heavens will pass away with a great noise, and the elements will melt with fervent heat**).

i. God *could* destroy the earth again as He did in the days of the flood. "There is still *water* enough to drown the earth, and there is *iniquity* enough to induce God to destroy it and its inhabitants." (Clarke) Yet God has promised to deal with this world with *fire*, not *flooding*.

B. Living in light of the last days and God's promise.

1. (11-13) Holy and godly living in anticipation of a new created order.

Therefore, since all these things will be dissolved, what manner *of persons* ought you to be in holy conduct and godliness, looking for and hastening the coming of the day of God, because of which the heavens will be dissolved, being on fire, and the elements will melt with fervent heat? Nevertheless we, according to His promise, look for new heavens and a new earth in which righteousness dwells.

a. **Therefore, since all these things will be dissolved, what manner of persons ought you to be**: In light of the fact that this world order and the things associated with it will be dissolved, we should live our lives seeking first the Kingdom of God and its righteousness – that is, having holy conduct and godliness.

i. We tend to think that the world is more enduring and will last longer than *people*. This is not true, and Peter reminds us of it. *People* will live into eternity, longer than even the earth.

ii. **Will be dissolved**: "They will all be *separated*, all *decomposed*; but none of them *destroyed*." (Clarke) "The solar system and the great galaxies, even space-time relationships, will be abolished . . . All elements which make up the physical world will be dissolved by heat and utterly melt away. It is a picture which in an astonishing degree corresponds to what might actually happen according to modern theories of the physical universe." (Bo Reicke, cited in Green)

iii. "This world, so far as we know, will not cease to be; it will pass through the purifying flame, and then it may be the soft and gentle breath of Almighty love will blow upon it and cool it rapidly, and the divine hand will shape it as it cools into a paradise more fair." (Spurgeon)

iv. **What manner of persons ought you to be**: "The king is coming; he is coming to his throne, and to his judgment. Now a man does not go up to a king's door, and there talk treason; and men do not sit in a king's audience-chamber when they expect him every moment to enter, and there speak ill of him. The King is on his way, and almost here; you are at his door; he is at yours. What manner of people ought ye to be? How can ye sin against One who is so close at hand?" (Spurgeon)

b. **Looking for and hastening the coming of the day of God**: Peter says there is a sense in which we can *hasten* the Lord's coming. It's remarkable to think that we can actually *do* things that will affect the return of Jesus. In the immediate context, Peter says that we hasten the Lord's coming by our **holy conduct and godliness**.

i. We can also hasten the Lord's coming through *evangelism*. Paul said that God's prophetic focus on Israel will resume when the *fullness of the Gentiles has come in* (Romans 11:25).

ii. We can also hasten the Lord's coming through *prayer*. Even as Daniel asked for a speedy fulfillment of prophecy regarding captive Israel (Daniel 9), we can also pray *"Even so, come, Lord Jesus!"* (Revelation 22:20).

c. **Because of which the heavens will be dissolved**: Peter tells us that the very elements of this world order **will be dissolved**. God will genuinely make a **new heavens and a new earth**, even as Isaiah promised: *For behold, I create new heavens and a new earth; and the former shall not be remembered or come to mind* (Isaiah 65:17).

d. **A new earth in which righteousness dwells**: The most glorious characteristic of this new heaven and new earth is that it is a place **in which righteousness dwells**. In God's plan of the ages, this happens after the millennial earth ruled by Jesus Christ.

i. It is the re-creation of this world order as described in Revelation 21:1: *"Now I saw a new heaven and a new earth, for the first heaven and the first earth had passed away."*

2. (14-15a) Keep diligent and do not despise the longsuffering of God.

Therefore, beloved, looking forward to these things, be diligent to be found by Him in peace, without spot and blameless; and consider *that* the longsuffering of our Lord *is* salvation;

a. **Looking forward to these things, be diligent**: If our hearts are really set on the glory of the new heaven and new earth, we will endeavor to walk godly in regard to our brothers and sisters (**in peace**) and in regard to God (**without spot and blameless**).

b. **The longsuffering of our Lord is salvation**: It is easy for Christians to sometimes resent the **longsuffering of God**; after all, it in some sense delays His coming. Yet, **the longsuffering of our Lord is salvation** for others, and it is salvation for us.

i. "We are puzzled at the longsuffering which causes so weary a delay. One of the reasons is that we have not much longsuffering ourselves. We think that we do well to be angry with the rebellious, and so we prove ourselves to be more like Jonah than Jesus. A few have learned to be patient and pitiful to the ungodly, but many more are of the mind of James and John, who would have called fire from heaven upon those who rejected the Savior. We are in such a hurry." (Spurgeon)

3. (15b-16) A note regarding the letters of the Apostle Paul.

As also our beloved brother Paul, according to the wisdom given to him, has written to you, as also in all his epistles, speaking in them of these things, in which are some things hard to understand, which untaught and unstable *people* twist to their own destruction, as *they do* also the rest of the Scriptures.

a. **As also our beloved brother Paul**: It is fashionable for some critics to say that the Apostle Peter and the Apostle Paul aren't in agreement. These same critics also often say that Peter and Paul aren't in agreement with Jesus. Yet here Peter affirmed Paul's teaching in the warmest terms. He called Paul **beloved** and said that Paul wrote with **wisdom**.

i. This praise from Peter is even more wonderful when we remember that at one time Paul publicly rebuked Peter for public compromise (Galatians 2:11-21).

b. **In which are some things hard to understand**: Though Peter praised Paul's ministry, he admitted that some things in Paul's writings were **hard to understand**, and those who were **untaught and unstable** could use some of the difficulties to their own ends, twisting Scripture.

c. **Twist . . . the Scriptures**: Peter reminds us that the Scriptures *can be* twisted. Just because someone quotes the Bible doesn't mean that they teach Biblical truth. It's possible that they **twist . . . the Scriptures**. That is why we should be like the Bereans, who *"searched the Scriptures daily to find out whether these things were so"* (Acts 17:11).

i. "It is worthy of remark that Paul's epistles are ranked among the *Scriptures*; a term applied to those writings which are divinely inspired, and to those only." (Clarke)

ii. "I may just add that the verb [**twist**], which the apostle uses here, signifies to *distort*, to *put to the rack*, to *torture*, to *overstretch*, and *dislocate the limbs*; and hence the persons here intended are those who proceed according to no fair plan of interpretation, but *force unnatural* and *sophistical meanings* on the word of God." (Clarke)

iii. **Destruction**: "Peter is very firm. The action of the false teachers in twisting Paul to justify their own libertinism and rejection of the parousia is so serious as to disqualify them from salvation." (Green)

4. (17-18) Conclusion.

You therefore, beloved, since you know *this* beforehand, beware lest you also fall from your own steadfastness, being led away with the error of the wicked; but grow in the grace and knowledge of our Lord and Savior Jesus Christ. To Him *be* the glory both now and forever. Amen.

a. **Since you know this beforehand**: We, who know of the Day of the Lord and await it with patient expectation, must persevere lest we **fall from your own steadfastness**. We must take care to keep abiding in Jesus.

i. "In order that they might know how to stand, and to be preserved from falling, he gave them this direction: 'grow in grace;' for the way to stand is to grow; the way to be steadfast is to go forward. There is no standing except by progression." (Spurgeon)

b. **But grow in the grace and knowledge of our Lord and Savior Jesus Christ**: We prevent a **fall from your own steadfastness** by a continual growth in **grace and knowledge of** Jesus.

i. **Grace** is not merely the way God draws us to Him in the beginning. It is also the way we grow and stay in our **steadfastness**. We can never grow apart from **the grace and knowledge of our Lord**, and we never grow out of God's grace.

ii. "But you will remark that our text does not say anything about grace growing; it does not say that grace grows. It tells us to 'grow in grace.' There is a vast difference between grace growing and our growing in grace. God's grace never increases; it is always infinite, so it cannot be more; it is always everlasting; it is always bottomless; it is always shoreless. It cannot be more; and, in the nature of God, it could not be less. The text tells us to 'grow in grace.' We are in the sea of God's grace; we cannot be in a deeper sea, but let us grow now we are in it." (Spurgeon)

iii. We must also grow in our **knowledge** of Jesus Christ. This means knowing more *about* Jesus, but more importantly, *knowing Jesus* in a personal relationship.

c. **To Him be the glory**: When we are this ready and this steadfast in the **grace and knowledge of our Lord**, it gives God glory.

i. Spurgeon noted that this second letter of Peter ends on "two trumpet blasts." One is from heaven to earth: **grow in the grace and knowledge of our Lord and Savior Jesus Christ**. The other is from earth to heaven: **To Him be the glory both now and forever**.

ii. **Amen**: This final word in not included in all ancient manuscripts of 2 Peter, yet it is appropriate for a letter affirming the truth in the face of the danger of false prophets and scoffers. We can say there are four meanings to "Amen":

- It expresses the *desire of the heart*.
- It expresses the *affirmation of our faith*.
- It expresses the *joy of the heart*.
- It expresses the *declaration of resolution*.

iii. Under the law, **Amen** was only said at the declaration of the *curses* (Deuteronomy 27:14-26). Under the New Covenant, we say "Amen" at the announcement of a great blessing and praise to God.

Adam Clarke added this insightful postscript to Second Peter:

"We have now passed over all the canonical writings of Peter that are extant; and it is worthy of remark that, in no place of the two epistles already examined, nor in any of this apostle's sayings in any other parts of the sacred writings, do we find any of the *peculiar* tenets of the Romish Church: not one word of *his* or the *pope's supremacy*; not one word of those of affect to be his *successors*; nothing of the *infallibility* claimed by those pretended successors; nothing of *purgatory, penances, pilgrimages, auricular confession, power* of the *keys, indulgences, extreme unction, masses,* and *prayers for the dead*; and not one word on the most essential doctrine of the Romish Church, *transubstantiation.*" (Clarke)

The Books of James and 1-2 Peter
Selected Bibliography

This is a bibliography of books cited in the commentary. Of course, there are many other worthy books on James and 1-2 Peter, but these are listed for the benefit of readers who wish to research sources.

Adamson, James *The Epistle of James* (Grand Rapids, Michigan: Eerdmans, 1976)

Barclay, William *The Letters of James and Peter* (Philadelphia: The Westminster Press, 1976)

Blum, Edwin A. "1, 2 Peter" *The Expositor's Bible Commentary, Volume 12* (Grand Rapids, Michigan: Zondervan, 1981)

Burdick, Donald W. "James" *The Expositor's Bible Commentary, Volume 12* (Grand Rapids, Michigan: Zondervan, 1981)

Calvin, John "The Epistles of James and Jude" *Calvin's New Testament Commentaries, Volume 3* [Translator: A.W. Morrison] (Grand Rapids, Michigan: Eerdmans, 1972)

Calvin, John "The First and Second Epistles of St. Peter" *Calvin's New Testament Commentaries, Volume 12* [Translator: W.B. Johnston] (Grand Rapids, Michigan: Eerdmans, 1976)

Clarke, Adam *The New Testament of Our Lord and Saviour Jesus Christ, Volume II* (New York: Eaton & Mains, 1832)

Hart, J.H.A. "The First Epistle General of Peter" *The Expositor's Greek Testament, Volume V* (London: Hodder and Stoughton Limited)

Hiebert, D. Edmond *The Epistle of James – Tests of a Living Faith* (Chicago, Illinois: Moody Press, 1979)

Hiebert, D. Edmond *1 Peter* (Chicago, Illinois: Moody Press, 1984)

Green, Michael *The Second Epistle General of Peter and the General Epistle of Jude, an Introduction and Commentary* (Leicester, England: Inter-Varsity Press, 1987)

Grudem, Wayne *The First Epistle of Peter, an Introduction and Commentary* (Leicester, England: Inter-Varsity Press, 1988)

Meyer, F.B. *Our Daily Homily* (Westwood, New Jersey: Revell, 1966)

Meyer, F.B. *Tried by Fire – Expositions of the First Epistle of Peter* (Grand Rapids, Michigan: Zondervan, 1950)

Moo, Douglas J. *The Letter of James, an Introduction and Commentary* (Leicester, England: Inter-Varsity Press, 1985)

Morgan, G. Campbell *An Exposition of the Whole Bible* (Old Tappan, New Jersey: Revell, 1959)

Morgan, G. Campbell *Searchlights from the Word* (New York: Revell, 1926)

Oesterley, W.E. "The General Epistle of James" *The Expositor's Greek Testament, Volume IV* (London: Hodder and Stoughton Limited)

Orr, J. Edwin *Full Surrender* (London: Marshall, Morgan & Scott, 1951)

Poole, Matthew *A Commentary on the Holy Bible, Volume III: Matthew-Revelation* (London: Banner of Truth Trust, 1969, first published in 1685)

Ramm, Bernard *Protestant Christian Evidences* (Chicago, Illinois: Moody Press, 1959)

Spurgeon, Charles Haddon *The New Park Street Pulpit, Volumes 1-6* and *The Metropolitan Tabernacle Pulpit, Volumes 7-63* (Pasadena, Texas: Pilgrim Publications, 1990)

Strachan, R.H. "The Second Epistle General of Peter" *The Expositor's Greek Testament, Volume V* (London: Hodder and Stoughton Limited)

Trapp, John *A Commentary on the Old and New Testaments, Volume Five* (Eureka, California: Tanski Publications, 1997)

Wiersbe, Warren W. *The Bible Exposition Commentary, Volume 2* (Wheaton, Illinois: Victor Books, 1989)

Wuest, Kenneth S. "First Peter" and "In These Last Days" *Wuest's Word Studies in the Greek New Testament, Volume 2* (Grand Rapids, Michigan: Eerdmans, 1983)

This book saw its final preparation in the last days of the earthly life of our dear friend Bobbye Moore. This book is dedicated with great love and fondest remebrance of Bobbye, and her dear husband Tony who passed to glory several years before her. God bless you, Bobbye. You have made a tremendous differenence in many lives, especially for our family.

Once again I am in grateful debt to the proofreading and editorial help of Martina Patrick.

We use the same cover format and artwork for this commentary series, so continued thanks to Craig Brewer who created the cover and helped with the layout. Kara Valeri helped with graphic design. Gayle Erwin provided both inspiration and practical guidance. I am often amazed at the remarkable kindness of others, and thanks to all who give the gift of encouragement. With each year that passes, faithful friends and supporters become all the more precious. Through all of you - and especially through my beloved Inga-Lill - God has been better to me than I have ever deserved.

After more than 20 years of pastoral ministry in California, David Guzik and his family moved to Europe to became the director of Calvary Chapel Bible College Germany in July of 2003.

David and his wife Inga-Lill live in Siegen, Germany. Their children Aan-Sofie, Nathan, and Jonathan live in Germany, Ireland, and the United States.

You can e-mail David at ewm@enduringword.com

For more resources by David Guzik, go to www.enduringword.com

Also by David Guzik

Verse-by-Verse Commentaries
Genesis (ISBN: 1-56599-049-8)
First Samuel (ISBN: 1-56599-040-4)
Second Samuel (ISBN: 1-56599-038-2)
Daniel (ISBN: 1-56599-036-6)
The Gospel of Mark (ISBN: 1-56599-035-8)
Acts (ISBN: 1-56599-047-1)
Romans (ISBN: 1-56599-041-2)
First Corinthians (ISBN: 1-56599-045-5)
Second Corinthians (ISBN: 1-56599-042-0)
Galatians and Ephesians (ISBN: 1-56599-034-X)
Philippians and Colossians (ISBN: 1-56599-029-3)
Hebrews (ISBN: 1-56599-037-4)
James and 1-2 Peter (ISBN: 1-56599-028-5)
1-2-3 John and Jude (ISBN: 1-56599-031-5)
Revelation (ISBN: 1-56599-043-9)

On Christian Living
Standing in Grace (ISBN: 1-56599-030-7)

Devotionals
Free and Clear (ISBN: 1-56599-033-1)
Near and True (ISBN: 1-56599-032-3)

Software
New Testament & More (ISBN: 1-56599-048-X)
This CD-ROM gives immediate access to thousands of pages of verse-by-verse Bible commentary through all of the New Testament and many Old Testament books. For ease of use, commentary is available in both Acrobat and HTML format. Also includes bonus audio resources - hours of David Guzik's teaching in mp3 format

Find audio teaching by David Guzik at
www.enduringword.com

CPSIA information can be obtained at www.ICGtesting.com
Printed in the USA
LVOW11s1242230115

424054LV00001B/308/P